THE
WURST!

THE
WURST!

THE VERY BEST OF GERMAN FOOD

OTTO WOLFF

Smith
Street
Books

CONTENTS

INTRODUCTION

This is not a book about sausages – although recipes for making weisswurst (page 12), mettwurst (page 16) and bratwurst (page 19) are rightfully included. Instead, this is a book that celebrates the very best of all German food – from street snacks, sides and salads to larger dishes, sweet baked goods and desserts. German food has a rich culinary history – as deep and important as French or Italian food – which this book explores.

These days, the influence of German cuisine stretches far beyond its borders. Classics, such as sauerkraut, pretzels, potato dumplings, strudel and Black Forest cake are commonplace in restaurants the world over, and street-food staples, such as the magnificent currywurst (page 25) – one of Germany's favourite 'fast foods' – can be found on the streets of most major cities across the globe.

The recipes in this book celebrate these authentic dishes as well as the everyday food made in homes across Germany: comfort-food dishes, such as warming soups, stews and roasts for cold winter days, hearty rich meatballs and schnitzels for sharing with friends, lighter dishes, such as Germany's answer to pasta – the famous spätzle – and let's not forget the humble sausage with its myriad flavours and toppings, which is so much more satisfying when made at home.

These dishes have been part of the German cooking repertoire for many decades, with some stretching back centuries. *The Wurst!* honours these traditional recipes and celebrates the tried-and-true classics – dishes that have been loved (and in and out of favour) for generations.

Go to any city in Germany and you'll see a joyfully global food scene – Thai food, sushi, French baguettes, Italian toasted sandwiches – but it is still the classics that you'll find made in home kitchens across the country: pretzels, sausages, currywurst, flammkuchen and butterbrot.

Look inside *The Wurst!* and discover the best of German cuisine.

CHAPTER ONE

SNACKS & SMALL DISHES

WEISSWURST

WHITE SAUSAGE

makes about 2.3 kg (5 lbs) poached sausages

---

1 kg (2 lb 3 oz) veal, cut into 2 cm (¾ in) cubes, chilled

1 kg (2 lb 3 oz) pork shoulder or belly, cut into 2 cm (¾ in) cubes, chilled

400 g (14 oz) pork fat, cut into 2 cm (¾ in) cubes, chilled

4 lengths natural pork sausage casings

handful flat-leaf parsley, finely chopped

50 g (1¾ oz/½ cup) powdered milk

50 g (1¾ oz) salt

3 teaspoons finely grated lemon zest

2 teaspoons ground white pepper

2 teaspoons ground yellow mustard seeds

1 teaspoon ground celery seeds

1 teaspoon onion powder

140 g (5 oz/1 cup) crushed ice

These classic sausages – little seen outside Bavaria – are eaten as a snack between breakfast and lunch (and often served with a morning beer!).

Ensure that your utensils and the veal, pork and fat are very cold before grinding. Once completely chilled, transfer to a large bowl.

Meanwhile, soak the casings in cold water for 30 minutes. If they are packed in salt, rinse thoroughly inside and out before soaking.

Assemble the meat grinder, using the medium plate.

Combine the parsley, powdered milk, salt, lemon zest, white pepper, mustard seeds, celery seeds and onion powder in a bowl. Sprinkle evenly over the cold meat and fat and mix well with your hands. Pass the meat twice through the grinder into a mixing bowl, gradually adding three-quarters of the ice to the grinder as you go.

Form a small patty from the sausage filling and cook in a small frying pan to test the seasoning. It may taste a little salty, but this will mellow on resting. Adjust the seasoning if necessary, then return the meat to the freezer. Fit the fine plate onto the meat grinder, then when assembled pass the filling through again along with the remaining ice.

Half-fill a large saucepan with water and place it over medium heat. Do not let it boil.

Fit the large sausage filler fitting to the machine and wet with water. Feed the casing on to the fitting, leaving the end open and a 10 cm (4 in) overhang to allow air to pass through. Do not tie the end at this stage. Sprinkle water on a clean baking tray and place under the filler fitting for the sausage to coil onto. Feed the ground meat through the machine taking care to fill the casing evenly without overfilling or stretching it. Leave a little room to twist the casing to form individual sausages every 15 cm (6 in). Tie both ends with individual knots.

Transfer the prepared sausages to the saucepan and reduce the heat to low. Poach over low heat until the internal temperature of the sausages reaches 72°C (162°F). Plunge the weisswurst into a bowl of iced water to stop the cooking process, adding more iced water until they are completely cold. Drain and pat dry, then pack into airtight containers and refrigerate for up to 2 days. Alternatively, pack in a single layer and freeze for up to 3 months.

LEBERKÄSE

GERMAN MEAT LOAF

serves 6

---

400 g (14 oz) minced (ground) beef, chilled
400 g (14 oz) minced (ground) pork, chilled
2 teaspoons cornflour (cornstarch)
10 g (⅓ oz) sea salt flakes
1 teaspoon sweet paprika
1 teaspoon ground white pepper
1 teaspoon Instacure #1 or Prague powder #1 (see note)
2 medium onions, chopped
140 g (5 oz/1 cup) crushed ice
200 g (7 oz) rindless streaky bacon, very finely chopped
1 tablespoon marjoram leaves, finely chopped
melted butter, for greasing

This deliciously moreish meat loaf has its German origins in the southern end of the country, but can also be found in various forms in Austria and Switzerland – and is a relative (of sorts) of the ubiquitous bologna sausage. You can serve the loaf in finger-thick slices with mild German mustard, Sauerkraut (page 63) and Brezeln (page 38), or in thin slices with pickled cucumbers between a crunchy bread roll.

Ensure that the meat is well chilled and stays cold throughout the preparation process.

Combine the cornflour, salt, paprika, pepper and curing powder in a mixing bowl.

In a food processor, blitz the beef, pork, cornflour mixture and onion, adding the ice gradually until a smooth paste forms. Transfer to a mixing bowl and add the bacon and marjoram. Mix well to combine. Cover the bowl and set aside in the fridge to cool for 30 minutes.

Preheat the oven to 180°C (350°F).

Brush butter on the base and sides of a loaf (bar) tin. Transfer to the fridge or freezer to chill for about 20 minutes.

Pack the chilled meat mixture into the tin. Smooth the top and deeply score lines to create a diamond pattern.

Bake for 45–60 minutes, until the top of the leberkäse is crisp and golden brown.

Note:

• *Curing powder is available online or from specialty stores.*

METTWURST

SMOKED SAUSAGE

makes about 2.2 kg (5 lb) smoked and cured sausages

1.5 kg (3 lb 5 oz) pork shoulder,
   cut into 2 cm (¾ in) cubes
1 kg (2 lb 3 oz) beef blade or chuck,
   cut into 2 cm (¾ in) cubes
500 g (1 lb 2 oz) pork fat, cut into
   2 cm (¾ in) cubes
4 lengths natural pork sausage
   casings
2 garlic cloves
60 g (2 oz) salt
1 tablespoon ground white pepper
2 teaspoons whole yellow
   mustard seeds
½ teaspoon ground nutmeg
½ teaspoon ground allspice
1 teaspoon Instacure #2 or Prague
   powder #2 or Kwikurit (see note
   on page 17)

There's no denying that it takes time and effort to make and smoke your own mettwurst – one of Germany's most loved foods – but the reward is one of the best-tasting sausages you will ever experience!

Ensure that your utensils and the pork, beef and fat are very cold before grinding. It helps to place the diced meat in the freezer for up to 1 hour and the pork fat for up to 2 hours. Once completely chilled, transfer to a large bowl and mix well with your hands.

Meanwhile, soak the casings in cold water for 30 minutes. If they are packed in salt, rinse thoroughly inside and out before soaking.

Assemble the meat grinder using the large plate. Pass the meat and fat through the grinder into a mixing bowl. Set aside in the fridge.

Pound the garlic and salt using a mortar and pestle to a paste. Add to the coarsely ground meat along with the pepper, mustard seeds, nutmeg, allspice and curing powder. Mix well with your hands for 3–4 minutes.

Fit the large sausage filler fitting to the machine and wet with water. Feed the casing on to the fitting, leaving the end open and a 10 cm (4 in) overhang to allow air to pass through. Do not tie the end at this stage. Sprinkle water on a clean baking tray and place under the filler fitting for the sausage to coil onto.

Feed the chilled meat through the machine taking care to fill the casing evenly without overfilling or stretching it. Leave a little room to twist the casing to form individual sausages every 20 cm (8 in). Tie both ends with individual knots and hang the sausages until dry to the touch before smoking. Applying smoke before they are dry will cause white patches to form on the casings. In humid weather, you can speed up the drying time by using an electric fan.

Using an electric or gas smoker cabinet, smoke the sausages at 50°C (120°F) for 8 hours, then increase the temperature to 65°C (150°F) for a further 1 hour.

Plunge the hot sausages into a basin of iced water to stop the cooking process. Hang the sausages up indoors, allowing the air to circulate, for 2 hours. Pack into airtight containers and store in the fridge for up to 4 days. Alternatively, pack in a single layer and freeze for up to 3 months.

BRATWURST

GERMAN GRILLED SAUSAGE

makes about 3.5 kg (7 lb 12 oz) raw sausages

2 kg (4 lb 6 oz) pork shoulder, cut
into 2 cm (¾ in) chunks, chilled
1 kg (2 lb 3 oz) veal, cut into 2 cm
(¾ in) cubes, chilled
500 g (1 lb 2 oz) pork fat, cut into
2 cm (¾ in) cubes, chilled
4 lengths natural pork sausage
casings
70 g (2½ oz) salt
1 tablespoon chopped marjoram
1½ teaspoons ground white pepper
1 teaspoon mustard powder
1 teaspoon ground allspice
1 teaspoon onion powder
¼ teaspoon ground ginger
210 g (7½ oz/1½ cups) crushed ice

The iconic bratwurst sausage – its name derived from Old German meaning 'chopped meat' – is most commonly made from pork or a combination of pork and veal (as in this recipe). A staple of the cuisine, it forms the basis of many classic dishes, including Currywurst (page 25).

Ensure that your utensils and the pork, veal and fat are very cold before grinding. It helps to place the diced meat in the freezer for up to 1 hour and the pork fat for up to 2 hours. Once completely chilled, transfer to a large bowl.

Meanwhile, soak the casings in cold water for 30 minutes. If they are packed in salt, rinse thoroughly inside and out before soaking.

Assemble the meat grinder, using the medium plate.

Combine the salt, marjoram, pepper, mustard powder, allspice, onion powder and ginger in a bowl, then sprinkle evenly over the cold meat and fat. Mix well with your hands, then pass the mixture twice through the grinder, adding the ice gradually to the mixer, into a mixing bowl.

Form a small patty from the sausage filling and cook in a small frying pan to test the seasoning. It may taste a little salty, but this will mellow on resting. Adjust the seasoning if necessary. Return the meat to the freezer while you prepare the machine to fill the sausages.

Fit the large sausage filler fitting to the machine and wet with water. Feed the casing on to the fitting, leaving the end open and a 10 cm (4 in) overhang to allow air to pass through. Do not tie the end at this stage. Sprinkle water on a clean baking tray and place under the filler fitting for the sausage to coil onto.

Feed the chilled, seasoned meat through the machine taking care to fill the casing evenly without overfilling or stretching it. Leave a little room to twist the casing to form individual sausages every 15 cm (6 in). Tie both ends with individual knots and hang the sausages to air-dry for 20–30 minutes before packing into airtight containers and refrigerating for up to 3 days. Alternatively, pack in a single layer and freeze for up to 3 months.

Serve the bratwurst with fried onion in long, crusty white rolls with Bavarian seeded mustard slathered on top.

BUTTERBROT

OPEN SANDWICHES

serves 4

---

butter, for spreading
3 slices light rye sourdough
3 slices dark rye sourdough

DAS KASEBROT

3 slices Allgäuer Emmentaler
   (similar to Emmental), sliced
   in half
2 dill pickles, sliced

DAS WÜRSTBROT

60 g (2 oz) liverwürst
2 tablespoons sweet fruit chutney

LEBERKÄSE

3 slices Leberkäse (page 15), sliced
   in half
2 teaspoons German mustard

Butterbrot – literally 'butter bread' – describes a whole range of recipes, which are (unsurprisingly) single slices of bread, spread with butter and topped with a few ingredients. For Germans, it's all about the bread – so seek out the best-quality rye sourdough and let the ingredients do all the hard work.

Generously butter the bread. Top the bread with each of the toppings, allowing two slices of bread for each topping variation. Cut the bread in half and serve on a platter for sharing.

LEBERKÄSE (TOP RIGHT)
DAS KASEBROT (BOTTOM RIGHT)
DAS WÜRSTBROT (BOTTOM LEFT)

CURRYWURST

CURRY SAUSAGE

serves 4

---

1 tablespoon vegetable oil
1 small white onion, finely chopped
1 garlic clove, crushed
1 tablespoon mild curry powder,
  plus extra to serve
600 ml (20½ fl oz) tomato passata
  (puréed tomatoes)
80 ml (2½ fl oz/⅓ cup) white wine
  vinegar
80 g (2¾ oz/⅓ cup) granulated
  sugar
2 teaspoons worcestershire sauce
2 teaspoons salt
2 teaspoons sweet paprika
1 teaspoon mustard powder
4 Bratwurst sausages (page 19)
hot chips/fries, to serve

Currywurst is undoubtedly one of Germany's most beloved 'fast foods'. It's a simple dish of thickly sliced sausages liberally doused in sauce and curry powder – and makes the perfect accompaniment to beer. Famously created by Herta Heuwer in Berlin in 1949, who was introduced to curry powder by British soldiers, the iconic status of currywurst has only grown in the prevailing decades since.

Heat the oil in a saucepan over medium–low heat and add the onion. Cook for 3–4 minutes until soft and translucent. Add the garlic and cook for a further 2 minutes, making sure the garlic doesn't burn. Add the curry powder and cook, stirring, for 1 minute before adding the tomato passata. Heat until simmering, then add the vinegar, sugar, worcestershire sauce, salt, paprika and mustard powder.

Simmer, uncovered, for 15 minutes or until thickened. Remove from the heat and process with a hand-held blender until smooth.

Preheat a chargrill (griddle) pan over high heat.

Cook the sausages on the pan for about 20 minutes until cooked through. To serve, cut the sausages into thick slices. Transfer to serving plates and spoon the sauce over the top. Sprinkle with extra curry powder and serve with hot chips on the side. Enjoy immediately with a glass of ice-cold German beer.

BAUERNFRÜHSTÜCK

FARMER'S BREAKFAST

serves 4

3 medium-sized potatoes
  (about 300 g/10½ oz), peeled
1 teaspoon olive oil
150 g (5½ oz) bacon slices, cut
  into thin strips
1 green capsicum (pepper),
  chopped
4 eggs
½ bunch chives, snipped,
  for garnish

Like some of the best breakfast dishes across the world, this 'farmer's breakfast' is also often eaten at lunch or dinner. It's a hearty dish that is similar to the American 'breakfast hash', or the British 'bubble and squeak'. Best of all, you don't need to be a farmer to eat it.

Place the potatoes in a saucepan and cover with water. Season with salt, then bring to the boil and cook for 15 minutes or until a knife slips through the flesh easily. Drain, allow to cool slightly, then slice the potatoes into rounds about 1 cm (½ in) thick.

Heat the olive oil in a large frying pan over medium–high heat and add the bacon and capsicum. Cook until the bacon is crisp and the capsicum is soft. Push the bacon and capsicum to one side of the pan, then add the sliced potato. Cook for 4–5 minutes on each side until lightly browned. Mix through the bacon and capsicum until the ingredients are evenly dispersed around the pan.

Preheat the grill (broiler) to high.

Whisk the eggs in a small bowl and season with salt and pepper. Pour into the pan and swirl, so that the egg evenly settles between the other ingredients. Reduce the heat to low, cover with a lid and cook for 3–5 minutes, until the egg is just set. Transfer the pan to the hot grill and cook for 3–4 minutes until brown on top. Garnish with the chopped chives and serve immediately.

KARTOFFELPUFFER

POTATO FRITTERS

makes 8 fritters

450 g (1 lb) medium-sized potatoes,
  peeled and grated
2 small onions, grated
¼ teaspoon salt
75 g (2¾ oz/½ cup) plain
  (all-purpose) flour
2 eggs, lightly beaten
125 ml (4 fl oz/½ cup) vegetable oil
4 mint sprigs

APPLE SAUCE

575 g (1 lb 4 oz) granny smith
  apples, peeled, cored and diced
¼ teaspoon ground cinnamon
pinch of salt
25 g (1 oz) sugar
squeeze of lemon juice

These addictive fried potato fritters, served with apple sauce, are a staple German street food and are often found at festivals throughout the country. If you prefer, you can also serve these fritters with blueberry jam, rather than the apple sauce.

To make the apple sauce, place all of the ingredients and 80 ml (2¾ fl oz/⅓ cup) water in a small saucepan over medium heat. Bring to the boil, then reduce the heat to low, cover and leave to cook for 15–20 minutes, until the apple has completely broken down. Remove from the heat and set aside to cool. If you would like a smooth sauce, place in a blender and blend until smooth. For a chunkier sauce, just mash with a fork until the larger chunks have broken down.

Combine the potato, onion, salt and flour in a bowl. Add the egg and mix well.

Heat the oil in a large frying pan over medium–high heat.

Fill a ⅓ measuring cup with the potato mixture and place the mixture in the pan. Flatten with the back of a spatula until the fritter is about 1.5 cm (½ in) thick. Repeat this process, until you have 3–4 fritters in the pan. Fry for 3–4 minutes on each side, until golden brown and cooked through. Transfer to paper towel to drain, then repeat with the remaining mixture.

Serve the fritters with warm or cold apple sauce on the side and garnish with mint leaves. Any leftover apple sauce will keep in an airtight container in the fridge for up to 1 week.

FISCHBRÖTCHEN

FISH AND SALAD ROLLS

makes 8 rolls

---

60 ml (2 fl oz/¼ cup) vegetable oil
8 small crusty white bread rolls
8 butter or red lettuce leaves
4–6 dill cucumbers, sliced
  lengthways, about 3 mm
  (¼ in) thick
½ quantity Brathering (page 34)
1 red onion

REMOULADE

2 tablespoons egg mayonnaise
1 tablespoon sour cream
1 teaspoon German mustard
2 tablespoons capers, chopped
2 tablespoons finely chopped dill
  pickles
2 tablespoons fresh soft herbs,
  such as flat-leaf parsley, dill,
  chives, marjoram or sorrel,
  finely chopped

FISHCAKES

185 ml (6 fl oz/¾ cup) full-cream
  (whole) milk
250 g (9 oz) skinless white fish
  fillets, such as cod, rockling
  or whiting
2 medium-sized potatoes, peeled
  and chopped into 1 cm (½ in) dice
1 onion, grated
1 small carrot, grated
1 tablespoon finely chopped
  flat-leaf parsley
1 teaspoon finely grated lemon zest
sea salt flakes
ground white pepper
1 egg, beaten
50 g (1¾ oz/½ cup) dry
  breadcrumbs

Fischbrötchen are bread rolls stuffed with fish, often eaten from street vendors. Although you'll find this snack in various forms across the country, they are especially loved in Northern Germany, due in large part to its proximity to the North Sea. Do like the Germans, and pick the freshest crusty white bread rolls for this recipe.

To make the remoulade, combine all of the ingredients in a small bowl. Set aside for the flavours to infuse.

To make the fish cakes, heat the milk in a small saucepan over medium heat until simmering. Add the fish and poach in the milk for 8–10 minutes, turning once. Remove the fish from the milk and set aside to cool. Add the potato to the milk, then cover and simmer for 6–8 minutes, until a knife slips easily through the potato. Drain and discard the milk. Transfer the potato to a mixing bowl and mash with the back of a fork. Add the onion, carrot, parsley and lemon zest, and season with sea salt flakes and white pepper. Stir until combined, then flake the fish finely and stir into the potato mixture.

Divide the mixture into quarters and form into balls, pressing firmly to flatten slightly. Transfer to a plate, then cover and chill in the fridge for 30 minutes to firm up. Place the beaten egg and breadcrumbs in separate shallow bowls. When the fishcakes have chilled, dip them into the egg and coat in breadcrumbs.

Heat the oil in a frying pan over medium heat. Working in batches, add the fishcakes and fry for 3–4 minutes on each side, until golden brown. Remove from the pan and drain on paper towel.

Slice the bread rolls nearly all the way through and spread both sides with remoulade. Place a lettuce leaf on the base of each roll and add 2–3 slices of pickle. Add the fish cakes to four of the rolls and brathering to the remaining four rolls and finish with some freshly sliced red onion rings. Serve immediately.

BIER-KÄSEDIP

BEER AND CHEESE DIP

serves 6–8

1 tablespoon olive oil
10 g (⅓ oz) butter
125 g (4½ oz) trimmed bacon slices,
  cut into thin strips
1 onion, thinly sliced
1 garlic clove, crushed
100 g (3½ oz) camembert, rind on
60 g (2 oz/½ cup) grated Swiss
  cheese
60 g (2 oz/½ cup) grated smoked
  or vintage cheddar
1 tablespoon plain (all-purpose)
  flour
3 tablespoons panko breadcrumbs
2 spring onions (scallions), thinly
  sliced
80 ml (2½ fl oz/⅓ cup) German
  beer, any variety
pinch of smoked hot paprika
Brezeln, to serve (page 38)

This rich, oozy dip with bacon, three cheeses and beer is not for the timid. But if you're going to indulge, you might as well go all the way and serve it with a large, cold beer and plenty of fresh pretzels!

Preheat the oven to 180°C (350°F).

Heat the oil and butter in a large heavy-based frying pan over medium–high heat. Cook the bacon, onion and garlic, stirring frequently, for 8–10 minutes, until the bacon is lightly browned and the onion and garlic are golden. Remove from the heat and set aside to cool for 5 minutes.

Depending on the ripeness of the cheese, chop or mash the camembert (including the rind). Transfer to a large bowl and add the Swiss cheese, cheddar and flour. Toss to combine, then add the breadcrumbs, spring onion, beer and half of the bacon mixture. Spoon into a 500 ml (17 fl oz/2 cup) capacity ovenproof dish and scatter over the remaining bacon mixture and paprika. Bake for 20–25 minutes, until the cheese is melted and the top golden.

Serve immediately with the Brezeln.

BRATHERING

FRIED MARINATED HERRING

serves 4

8 fresh herring, scaled and gutted
  (alternatively, you can use
  sardines)
sea salt flakes
60 g (2 oz) plain (all-purpose) flour
60 ml (2 fl oz/¼ cup) olive oil

PICKLING LIQUID

1 large onion, sliced into rings
2 tablespoons yellow mustard seeds
1 tablespoon black peppercorns
1 tablespoon sea salt flakes
2 fresh bay leaves
250 ml (8½ fl oz/1 cup) white
  vinegar

Brathering – a popular dish of fresh herring that are first fried then pickled – is a traditional German snack often sold at street-food stands. If herring is difficult to come by, sardines make a great alternative.

To prepare the brathering, use kitchen scissors to remove the heads and tails from the fish. Wash the herring inside and out under cold running water, then pat dry. Sprinkle a little sea salt on both sides. Place the flour on a plate and dredge the fish in the flour, pressing to coat well.

Heat the oil in a frying pan over high heat. Working in batches, fry the fish for 2 minutes on each side. Remove from the pan and lay the fish in a single layer in a glass or ceramic dish.

To make the picking liquid, place 250 ml (8½ fl oz/1 cup) water, the onion, mustard seeds, peppercorns, salt and bay leaves in a saucepan over medium heat. Bring to the boil, then add the vinegar and return to the boil. Remove from the heat, allow to cool a little, then pour the marinade over the fish and set aside to cool completely. Cover and refrigerate for at least 3 days before eating. The bones will dissolve in the vinegar. The fish will keep in the fridge for 2–3 weeks.

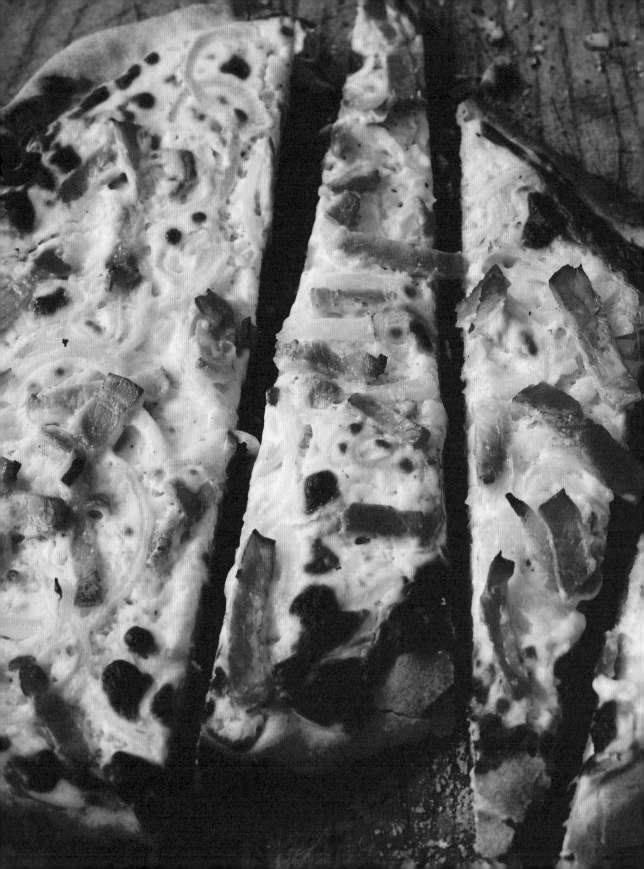

FLAMMKUCHEN

SAVOURY BAKED TARTS

makes 4

375 g (13 oz/1½ cups) quark or
  spreadable cream cheese
1–2 tablespoons full-cream (whole)
  milk (optional)
pinch of freshly grated nutmeg
1 onion, very thinly sliced
150 g (5½ oz) trimmed bacon slices,
  cut into thin strips

DOUGH

600 g (1 lb 5 oz/4 cups) plain
  (all-purpose) baker's flour, plus
  extra for dusting
2 teaspoons instant dried yeast
1 teaspoon salt
400 ml (13½ fl oz) warm water
2 tablespoons olive oil, plus extra
  for greasing

This is Germany's answer to pizza: a yeasted dough rolled out and topped with quark, bacon and nutmeg before baking until crisp. Traditionally, flammkuchen, as the literal translation of 'flame cake' suggests, is cooked in a wood-fired oven for a few short minutes – but at home a very hot oven will do the trick.

To make the dough, combine the flour, yeast and salt in a large bowl. Pour in the water and olive oil. Mix until combined to form a rough dough, then cover the bowl with plastic wrap and set aside for 10 minutes.

Turn the dough out onto a lightly floured work surface and knead for 4–5 minutes until quite smooth. Place in a clean bowl lightly oiled with olive oil, cover with plastic wrap and set aside in a warm place for 30–40 minutes until doubled in size.

Preheat the oven to 240°C (460°F).

Turn the dough out onto a lightly floured work surface and divide into quarters. Shape into balls and set aside to rest for 10 minutes. Working with one piece of dough at a time, roll out the dough until it is about 24 cm (9½ in) in diameter. Place on a large baking tray.

Gently whisk the quark or cream cheese with enough milk (if needed) to make a spreadable mixture. Stir in the nutmeg and season with salt and freshly ground black pepper.

Spread the dough with a quarter of the quark or cream cheese mixture, leaving a 1 cm (½ in) border around the edge. Scatter evenly with a quarter of the onion and a quarter of the bacon.

Bake for 8–10 minutes or until the base is crisp and cooked through and the top is very well browned, if not tinged in spots.

Serve immediately, then repeat with the remaining dough and toppings.

BREZELN MIT WEISSWURST

PRETZELS WITH WHITE SAUSAGE

serves 4

---

8 Weisswurst sausages, to serve
  (page 12)
German mustard, to serve

BREZELN

375 g (13 oz/2½ cups) plain
  (all-purpose) baker's flour,
  plus extra for dusting
2 teaspoons instant dried yeast
1 teaspoon salt
½ teaspoon mustard powder
pinch of cayenne pepper
250 ml (8½ fl oz/1 cup) warm water
olive oil, for greasing
70 g (2½ oz/¼ cup) bicarbonate
  of soda (baking soda)
1 tablespoon brown sugar
1 egg
sea-salt flakes or pretzel salt

The pretzel is so beloved and intrinsic to the culture in Germany that it has been a staple of bakeries for more than 800 years. Master making the pretzel and you're halfway to becoming German!

Line a large baking tray with baking paper.

Combine the flour, yeast, salt, mustard powder and cayenne in a large bowl. Add the warm water and mix until you have a rough, soft dough (adding a little extra warm water, if required). Cover the bowl with plastic wrap and set aside for 10 minutes.

Turn the dough out onto a lightly floured work surface and knead for 2–3 minutes until smooth. Place in a lightly oiled bowl, cover with plastic wrap and set aside in a warm place for about 1 hour or until doubled in size.

Turn the dough out again onto a lightly floured work surface and divide into 8 equal-sized pieces. Working with one piece of dough at a time, roll the dough against the work surface using the palms of your hands into a long, skinny rope, about 60 cm (24 in) in length. If the dough shrinks back, set it aside to rest while you work on another piece.

To shape the brezeln, lift the ends of one rope of dough towards the top of your work surface to make a 'u' shape and twist them together. Bring the twisted rope back down over the bottom loop to form a pretzel shape. Adhere lightly to the base of the loop and place on the prepared tray. Repeat with the remaining dough ropes, then cover loosely with plastic wrap and set aside for 20–30 minutes, until slightly risen.

Preheat the oven to 230°C (450°F). Pour 2 litres (64 fl oz/8 cups) water into a large wide pot and place over high heat. Bring to the boil, then gradually sprinkle in the bicarbonate of soda. It will foam up rapidly, so be careful. Add the sugar and stir to combine. Reduce the heat until the mixture is simmering.

Working in batches of 2–3 brezeln at a time, carefully add to the pan and simmer for 30 seconds. Flip the brezeln over and simmer for a further 30 seconds. Scoop the brezeln out with a slotted spoon, drain and return to the prepared tray. Whisk the egg with 2 tablespoons of water in a small bowl. Brush the brezeln with the egg mixture and sprinkle with salt.

Bake the brezeln for 12–15 minutes, until cooked through and deep brown. Serve with the weisswürst and mustard on the side. The brezeln are best eaten on the day they are made.

SENFEIER MIT BLATTSPINAT

MUSTARD EGGS WITH SPINACH

serves 4

---

6 eggs

MUSTARD SAUCE
50 g (1¾ oz) unsalted butter
35 g (1¼ oz/¼ cup) plain
   (all-purpose) flour
250 ml (8½ fl oz/1 cup) full-cream
   (whole) milk
250 ml (8½ fl oz/1 cup) vegetable
   or chicken stock
1 tablespoon German wholegrain
   (seeded) mustard
1 tablespoon smooth German
   mustard

SAUTÉED SPINACH
20 g (¾ oz) unsalted butter
1 tablespoon olive oil
1 large bunch spinach (about
   500 g/1 lb 2 oz), trimmed

This is a no-fuss traditional comfort-food dish that any German grandmother could whip up in no time at all. If you'd like to make this snack into a main meal, simply serve the eggs and spinach alongside some creamy mashed potato.

Bring a small saucepan of water to the boil over high heat. Reduce the heat to a simmer and lower the eggs into the water with a spoon. Simmer for 6 minutes for runny yolks or a little longer if you prefer firmer yolks. Drain the eggs and run under cold water until cool. Peel carefully and set aside.

To make the mustard sauce, melt the butter in a small heavy-based saucepan over medium heat until bubbling. Add the flour and cook, stirring, for 1–2 minutes, until it is the texture of wet sand.

Pour in the milk and stock, stirring continuously. Bring to the boil while continuing to stir, then reduce the heat and simmer for about 5 minutes or until thickened slightly. Remove from the heat and stir in the mustards. Season with salt and freshly ground black pepper, to taste.

To make the sautéed spinach, heat the butter and oil in a large frying pan over medium heat. Add the spinach and cook for 3–5 minutes, turning the spinach with tongs occasionally, until wilted. Season, to taste.

Carefully cut the eggs in half lengthways and serve with the spinach and mustard sauce.

GEBRANNTE MANDELN

ROASTED CINNAMON ALMONDS

makes 375 g (13 oz) almonds

320 g (11½ oz) sugar
1 vanilla bean, split lengthways
  and seeds scraped
2 teaspoons ground cinnamon
½ teaspoon salt
350 g (12½ oz/2¼ cups) almonds

These crunchy, cinnamon-laced almonds are a popular snack during the Christkindlmarkt (Christmas market) season, where they're sold in decorative paper cones. Be warned – they're extremely addictive.

Line a baking tray with baking paper.

Place 80 g (2¾ oz) of the sugar in a bowl. Add the vanilla seeds and mix with your hands until well combined. Set aside.

Place the cinnamon, salt, remaining sugar and 100 ml (3½ fl oz) water in a saucepan (do not use a non-stick pan) over high heat. Stir until the sugar and salt have dissolved. Add the almonds and continue to cook for 2–3 minutes, stirring continuously, until the water has evaporated – you should be left with a syrup that's still bubbling. Reduce the heat to low and continue to stir. The sugar will begin to cool and crystallise around the almonds, and they will turn pale in colour.

When the sugar mix has coated the almonds, add the reserved vanilla sugar and increase the heat to high again, stirring constantly, until the sugar at the bottom of the pan begins to melt. Continue to stir for 1–2 minutes, then remove the pan from the heat.

Transfer the coated almonds to the baking tray and allow to cool before serving in paper cones for that festival feel!

The almonds will keep in an airtight container for 3–4 weeks.

FRANZBRÖTCHEN

BUTTER AND CINNAMON PASTRIES

makes 12

500 g (1 lb 2 oz/3⅓ cups) plain
   (all-purpose) flour, plus extra
   for dusting
55 g (2 oz/¼ cup) caster
   (superfine) sugar
1½ teaspoons instant dried yeast
½ teaspoon salt
250 ml (8½ fl oz/1 cup) full-cream
   (whole) milk, warmed, plus extra
   for brushing
70 g (2½ oz) unsalted butter,
   melted and cooled
1 egg, beaten

FILLING

100 g (3½ oz) butter, softened
75 g (2¾ oz/⅓ cup) brown sugar
1 tablespoon ground cinnamon

Franzbrötchen are small sweet pastries, baked with butter and cinnamon (and sometimes with raisins and chocolate). Especially popular in Hamburg, they're usually eaten for breakfast alongside a strong coffee.

Combine the flour, sugar, yeast and salt in a large bowl. Pour in the milk, butter and egg and mix until it forms a rough dough. Cover the bowl with plastic wrap and set aside for 10 minutes.

Turn the dough out onto a lightly floured work surface and knead for 2–3 minutes until smooth. Place in a lightly oiled bowl, cover with plastic wrap and set aside in a warm place for 45–60 minutes until risen by half its original size.

Preheat the oven to 180°C (350°C). Line a large baking tray with baking paper.

To make the filling, combine the butter, sugar and cinnamon in a small bowl.

Turn the dough out again onto a lightly floured work surface and gently roll out to a rectangle about 60 cm x 25 cm (24 in x 10 in). Spread the dough with the butter mixture and, starting with a long edge, roll the dough firmly into a spiral. Cut into 12 equal-sized slices.

Place the dough slices on the prepared tray, seam side down, about 5 cm (2 in) apart. Using a thin wooden spoon handle (or a chopstick), press down on top of the dough to make a dip in the middle, pushing out the cut sides so that the spirals face upwards slightly. Set aside, covered loosely with plastic wrap, for 10 minutes or until slightly risen.

Brush the rolls gently with the extra milk and bake for 20–25 minutes, until lightly browned and cooked through. Serve warm or cool. The pastries are best eaten on the day they are made.

SPRITZKUCHEN

CRULLERS

makes about 12

---

50 g (1¾ oz) butter
2 tablespoons sugar
200 g (7 oz/1⅓ cups) plain
   (all-purpose) flour
4–5 eggs
1 teaspoon vanilla extract
vegetable oil for deep-frying,
   plus extra for brushing

ICING

125 g (4½ oz/1 cup) icing
   (confectioners') sugar
2 tablespoons full-cream
   (whole) milk
55 g (2 oz/¼ cup) fresh mixed
   berries, such as red currants,
   raspberries or blackberries

Spritzkuchen are a little like German donuts: an egg-rich dough shaped into a circle and fried in hot oil until golden. If you like, skip the icing and dust the Spritzkuchen with cinnamon sugar.

To make the dough, place the butter, sugar and 250 ml (8½ fl oz/1 cup) water in a saucepan over low heat and heat until the butter has melted.

Add the flour and stir with a wooden spoon until you have a thick, smooth dough. Remove from the heat and transfer to an electric mixer fitted with a paddle attachment.

Allow the dough to cool a little, then add 4 of the eggs one at a time, beating well after each addition. Add the vanilla with the fourth egg and beat well. The dough should be thick, sticky and smooth. Use a spoon to check the dough consistency: if the dough slides to the rim of the spoon, it is ready. If it is too firm, add the remaining egg and beat again.

Heat enough oil for deep-frying in a large saucepan until a breadcrumb starts to sizzle when dropped in.

Cut twenty 10 cm (4 in) squares of baking paper. Brush each square with a little oil. Transfer the dough to a piping (icing) bag fitted with a wide star nozzle and pipe a dough circle onto each square.

Slide 3–4 dough circles into the hot oil, top side down. Fry on each side for about 2 minutes, until golden. Remove from the pan and drain and cool on paper towel. Repeat with the remaining dough.

To make the icing, combine the icing sugar, milk and berries in a small bowl – the berries will break up on stirring and colour the icing. Drizzle the icing over the spritzkuchen and serve immediately. They are best eaten on the day they are made.

CHAPTER TWO

SALADS & SIDES

GURKENSALAT

CUCUMBER SALAD

serves 4–6 as a side

---

2 long (telegraph) cucumbers
1 teaspoon salt
½ red onion, thinly sliced
1 small bunch dill, chopped

DRESSING

60 ml (2 fl oz/¼ cup) white vinegar
pinch of sugar
1 teaspoon celery salt
200 g (7 oz) sour cream

This classic German salad is often served alongside roasted or barbecued meats. Salting the cucumber slices draws out the moisture and enhances their crunchy texture.

Peel one of the cucumbers, then slice both cucumbers as thinly as possible.

Place the cucumber in a bowl, then add the salt and toss to combine. Set aside for 30–60 minutes, then drain away the excess liquid, lightly squeezing the cucumber to release excess moisture. Transfer to a clean bowl, add the red onion and toss to combine.

To make the dressing, mix the vinegar, sugar, celery salt and sour cream in a small bowl until well combined. Season with freshly ground black pepper.

Pour the dressing over the cucumber and onion and sprinkle with the chopped dill. Toss to combine until the ingredients are evenly coated, then season to taste and serve immediately.

WEISSKRAUTSALAT

WHITE CABBAGE SALAD

serves 4–6 as a side

1 teaspoon caraway seeds
½ teaspoon sugar
60 ml (2 fl oz/¼ cup) apple cider
vinegar
170 ml (5½ fl oz/⅔ cup) vegetable
stock or water
½ small white cabbage (about
600 g/1 lb 5 oz), shredded
2 tablespoons extra virgin olive oil
freshly ground white pepper
handful chopped flat-leaf parsley
(optional)
handful shredded cooked ham
(optional)

Without a doubt, Germans love their cabbage! Weisskrautsalat is often served alongside Kartoffelsalat (page 55) with baked or roasted meats, chicken or fish dishes. Shred the cabbage with a mandoline, if you have one, or slice it thinly with a sharp knife.

Combine the caraway seeds, sugar, vinegar and stock or water in a small saucepan over medium heat. Bring to the boil, then remove from the heat.

Place the cabbage in a large heatproof bowl and pour over the hot vinegar mixture. Mix well and set aside for 15–20 minutes, stirring occasionally, until cooled and slightly softened. Drain and discard the liquid. Toss the drained cabbage with the oil and season well with salt and freshly ground white pepper. Serve, scattered with parsley and ham, if you like.

KARTOFFELSALAT

POTATO SALAD

serves 6 as a side

3 eggs
1 teaspoon olive oil
200 g (7 oz) bacon slices, cut
   into batons
1 kg (2 lb 3 oz) new potatoes
3 chicken stock cubes
½ red onion, thinly sliced
15 cornichons, sliced lengthways
1 small bunch flat-leaf parsley,
   chopped
1 small bunch chives, snipped

DRESSING

125 ml (4 fl oz/½ cup) olive oil
60 ml (2 fl oz/¼ cup) white wine
   vinegar
2 tablespoons dijon mustard
pinch of sugar

The mighty potato salad – a beloved dish across the world in its myriad variations – is believed to have originated in Germany. The country itself has different traditions – a mayonnaise dressing is more popular in the North, while a dressing of vinegar and oil (as with this recipe) is more favoured in the South. In either case, the potatoes are first cooked in stock to impart extra flavour in the dish.

In a small bowl, whisk together all of the ingredients for the dressing, season with salt and freshly ground black pepper and set aside.

Place the eggs in a small saucepan, cover with cold water and bring to the boil over high heat. Reduce to a rolling simmer and cook for 6 minutes. Remove from the heat and place the eggs directly into iced water. Once cool, peel and cut in half lengthways.

Heat the olive oil in a frying pan over high heat and add the bacon. Cook until crisp, then remove with a slotted spoon and set aside to drain on paper towel.

Place the potatoes in a large saucepan, cover with water and bring to the boil. Add the stock cubes and cook for about 15 minutes, or until a knife slips through the potatoes easily. Drain, then halve or quarter the potatoes depending on their size. Transfer to a large bowl and allow to cool for a few minutes. Add the red onion, bacon, cornichons, herbs and the dressing. Toss to combine until everything is evenly coated in the dressing, then add the eggs and gently combine. Serve warm.

SPÄTZLE

EGG NOODLES

serves 4–6

3 large eggs
½ teaspoon salt
pinch of ground nutmeg (optional)
300 g (10½ oz/2 cups) plain (all-purpose) flour
50 g (1¾ oz) unsalted butter, plus extra for greasing
handful chopped flat-leaf parsley

Spätzle is to Germany what pasta is to Italy – a hearty wheat-based noodle made with few ingredients and used as the base in many dishes.

Using a wooden spoon, combine the eggs, salt, nutmeg, if using, and 180 ml (6 fl oz/¾ cup) water in a large bowl. Add the flour and mix well until you have a smooth, thick and quite sticky batter (similar to a thick pancake batter). Cover and set aside to rest for 20 minutes. Adjust the consistency with a little more water or flour, if required.

Bring a large saucepan of water to the boil and add a good pinch of salt. Working in batches, pour some of the batter into a large-holed colander or spätzle press held above the boiling water. Scrape the batter with a spatula or press, to push little droplets or strands of batter through the colander and into the water. Gently stir the spätzle to prevent it from sticking. Cook until the spätzle float to the surface, then continue cooking for a further 1–2 minutes until cooked through. Using a slotted spoon, transfer the spätzle to a lightly buttered bowl, then repeat the process with the remaining batter.

Melt the butter in a large heavy-based frying pan over medium heat. Cook, swirling the pan for 2–3 minutes or until the butter is golden brown. Add the spätzle and toss in the butter until heated through. Scatter with parsley and season with salt and freshly ground black pepper. Serve immediately.

Tips:

- *The spätzle can be made up to 2 hours before serving.*
- *Let stand at room temperature.*

KÄSESPÄTZLE

CHEESE AND EGG NOODLES

serves 6

---

15 g (½ oz) butter, plus extra
  for greasing
1 tablespoon olive oil
1 onion, thinly sliced
1 quantity cooked Spätzle (page 56
  – without pan-frying in butter)
200 g (7 oz/1 cup) grated Allgäuer
  Emmentaler (or Swiss cheese or
  gruyère)

The ultimate German comfort food, Käsespätzle is essentially a simple-to-prepare mac 'n' cheese. If you've got a good local cheesemonger, search out the traditional German Allgäuer Emmentaler – a hard, unpasteurised cow's milk cheese.

Preheat the oven to 180°C (350°F). Lightly butter a 1 litre (34 fl oz/4 cup) shallow baking dish.

Heat the butter and oil in a large heavy-based frying pan over medium heat. Add the onion and season well with salt. Cook, stirring occasionally, for 6–8 minutes until golden. Set aside.

Toss the spätzle and cheese together in a large bowl. Transfer to the prepared dish and top with the onion. Bake for 20–25 minutes, until bubbling and lightly browned on top.

KÄSESPÄTZLE (RIGHT)
SPÄTZLE (LEFT)

SPÄTZLE UND SPARGELSALAT

EGG NOODLE AND ASPARAGUS SALAD

serves 4–6

½ small red onion, thinly sliced
2 tablespoons red wine vinegar
½ quantity cooked Spätzle (page 56
  – without pan-frying in butter)
1 teaspoon olive oil
1 bunch asparagus
20 g (¾ oz) butter
200 g (7 oz) mixed cherry
  tomatoes, halved

HERB VINAIGRETTE

finely grated zest and juice of
  1 lemon
1 tablespoon finely chopped fresh
  herbs, such as flat-leaf parsley,
  chives or oregano
½ small garlic clove, crushed
1 teaspoon caster (superfine)
  sugar (optional)
60 ml (2 fl oz/¼ cup) olive oil
60 ml (2 fl oz/¼ cup) red wine
  vinegar
freshly ground white pepper

This hearty noodle salad is rightfully popular in spring, when asparagus is at its peak. If available, substitute half the green asparagus for fresh white asparagus. It's delicious eaten on its own, or served alongside fish or chicken dishes.

To make the vinaigrette, put all of the ingredients in a jar. Pop the lid on and shake until well combined. Season with a little salt, then set aside for the flavours to mellow.

Combine the onion and vinegar in a small bowl and set aside.

In a large bowl, toss the spätzle with the olive oil and set aside.

Snap the woody ends off the asparagus and peel the bottom third of the spears if you like. Fill a large frying pan with water to a depth of about 2.5 cm (1 in) and bring to the boil. Add the butter and asparagus and cook for 2–3 minutes or until just tender. Remove with a slotted spoon and drain on paper towel.

Cut the asparagus into short lengths then add to the spätzle along with the tomato halves and half of the dressing. Toss to combine, then transfer to a serving platter. Drain the onion, discarding the vinegar, and scatter over the salad. Drizzle with the remaining dressing just before serving.

SAUERKRAUT

FERMENTED CABBAGE

makes about 600 g (1 lb 5 oz)

1 small (about 1 kg/2 lb 3 oz)
white cabbage
1 tablespoon fine sea salt (not
iodised)
1 teaspoon caraway seeds (optional)

Without a doubt, sauerkraut – a dish of fermented white cabbage – is one of Germany's most iconic recipes. This is a simple dish, but it does take time for the fermenting process to work its magic.

Sterilise a 1 litre (34 fl oz/4 cup) capacity jar and set aside.

Cut the cabbage in half and reserve one of the large, outer leaves. Remove the core and finely shred the cabbage. Transfer to a large bowl and sprinkle with the salt.

Using your hands, knead the salt into the cabbage, squeezing firmly to help release the liquid from the cabbage and reduce its volume by about half. This can take up to 10 minutes and there should be plenty of liquid in the bottom of the bowl. Add the caraway seeds, if using, and knead them in.

Pack the wilted cabbage into the prepared jar a few handfuls at a time, firmly pressing down after each addition to exclude any air from the mixture. Pour over the liquid left in the bowl – it should cover the cabbage with room to spare. Cut the reserved cabbage leaf so it fits snugly in the jar and press over the shredded cabbage to keep it submerged by at least 2 cm (¾ in). The liquid is likely to bubble over the lip of the jar. To help keep the cabbage submerged, add stone or glass weights if you have them, or you can use a small zip-lock bag filled with water.

Loosely cap the jar and place in a cool, dark spot (18–22°C/64–72°F is ideal). If the vessel is quite full, sit it on a plate or dish to catch any overflowing fluids.

Check the jar every second day, removing any bloom and pressing the cabbage down if it has floated above the liquid. It is very important that the cabbage always remains below the liquid level. If necessary, you can top the liquid up by diluting 2 g (⅛ oz) salt in 100 ml (3½ fl oz) water and adding it to the jar.

Taste the sauerkraut after one week. If you like the flavour, place the jar in the refrigerator. If you prefer a stronger taste, let it continue to ferment for a few more days. Depending on the temperature it can take up to 6 weeks to fully ferment. Refrigerate in the sealed jar for up to 6 months. Throw out the sauerkraut if it becomes discoloured, slimy or malodorous. (Some sulphurous smell is natural, but anything truly offensive is a bad sign!)

ROTKOHL

COOKED RED CABBAGE

serves 4 as a side

---

1 tablespoon olive oil
1 onion, finely chopped
500 g (1 lb 2 oz) red cabbage,
   finely chopped
1 large granny smith apple, peeled,
   cored and diced
4 juniper berries
5 cloves
1 teaspoon salt
½ teaspoon sugar
1 dried bay leaf
125 ml (4 fl oz/½ cup) apple juice
2 tablespoons red wine vinegar

Rotkohl is a classic German side dish, often served alongside hearty meat and poultry dishes, including Roast goose (page 86). The hot and sour cabbage helps to cut through the meat's richness.

Heat the olive oil in a saucepan over medium–high heat. Add the onion and fry for 4–5 minutes, stirring, until translucent but not browned.

Add the cabbage to the pan, stir to combine and fry for a further 2–3 minutes.

Add all of the remaining ingredients along with 125 ml (4 fl oz/½ cup) water and bring to the boil. Reduce the heat to low, cover with a lid and cook for 1¼–1½ hours. Stir occasionally and add a little water if it looks like the cabbage is catching on the base of the pan.

KARTOFFELKNÖDEL

POTATO DUMPLINGS

makes 8 dumplings

---

1 kg (2 lb 3 oz) medium-sized floury
  potatoes
1 teaspoon sea salt flakes
90 g (3 oz/¾ cup) potato flour
  or cornflour (cornstarch)
2 egg yolks
pinch of freshly grated nutmeg

**CROUTON AND PARSLEY
FILLING**

60 g (2 oz) butter
2 slices white sourdough bread,
  crusts removed and cut into
  small cubes
1 teaspoon chopped flat-leaf
  parsley

OR:

SPECK FILLING

1 tablespoon olive oil
250 g (9 oz) speck or smoked
  bacon, finely diced
1 small onion, finely chopped
1 teaspoon chopped flat-leaf
  parsley

Potato dumplings are popular across Germany, but especially in Bavaria, where they're served with many braised and roasted dishes. Be warned – these dumplings are so filling, you'll likely only need one per person.

To make the crouton filling, melt the butter in a frying pan over medium heat. Add the bread cubes and toast on all sides until golden brown. Drain on paper towel, then combine with the parsley.

To make the speck filling, heat the oil in a frying pan over medium heat. Add the speck and onion and cook, stirring occasionally, for 10 minutes or until the fat has rendered and the onion is golden brown. Set aside to cool a little, then combine with the parsley.

Boil the potatoes in plenty of salted boiling water for 10 minutes or until a knife slips easily through the potatoes. Drain, set aside to cool a little, then peel. Press the potatoes through a potato ricer over a heatproof bowl and set aside to cool completely. Mix the potato with the sea salt flakes, flour, egg yolks and nutmeg to form a dough. Divide the dough and your choice of filling evenly into 8 portions and use damp hands to form dumplings. Press a hole into each dumpling, and fill with the croutons and parsley or speck filling. Reshape until smooth.

Bring a large saucepan of salted water to a simmering boil over medium heat. Add the dumplings, in batches if necessary, and cook for 15–20 minutes, until the dumplings rise to the top of the pan – take care that the water does not boil, as the dumplings will disintegrate.

CHAPTER THREE
MAINS

FISCHEINTOPF

FISH STEW

serves 4–6

400 g (14 oz) firm white fish fillets, such as cod or whiting
juice of ½ lemon
½ teaspoon sea salt flakes
2 tablespoons olive oil
1 medium onion, chopped
2 medium carrots, chopped
2 celery stalks, chopped
1 medium zucchini (courgette), chopped
2 medium tomatoes, chopped
2 handfuls green beans, trimmed and chopped
80 ml (2½ fl oz/⅓ cup) white wine
500 ml (17 fl oz/2 cups) vegetable stock
2 medium potatoes, peeled and diced
small handful flat-leaf parsley, chopped
fresh rye bread, to serve

This hearty and chunky fish stew is a meal on its own, but it wouldn't be complete without some fresh rye bread for sopping up the delicious stock. Use any firm white fish you like, but ensure that all the skin is removed.

Rinse the fish and pat dry. Sprinkle with lemon juice and salt and set aside while you prepare the stew.

Heat the oil in a large saucepan over medium heat. Add the onion, carrot and celery and cook, stirring occasionally, for 5 minutes or until softened.

Add the zucchini, tomato and beans and cook for a further 5 minutes. Add the wine and stir to loosen any vegetables caught on the base of the pan. Add the stock and potato, season with freshly ground black pepper and place the marinated fish on top of the vegetables.

Cover the pan and simmer on medium–low heat for 20–25 minutes, until the potato is tender and the fish flakes easily when tested with a fork. Break up the fish into chunks, add the parsley and give everything a good stir.

Transfer the fischeintopf into deep bowls and serve with fresh rye bread.

HOCHZEITSSUPPE

WEDDING SOUP

serves 4 as a starter or 2 as a main

8 white asparagus stalks (from a jar
  is fine), each cut into 4 pieces
80 g (2¾ oz) fresh or frozen peas
1 carrot, diced
90 g (3 oz) pasta, such as casarecce
2 tablespoons chopped flat-leaf
  parsley, for garnish

BROTH

500 g (1 lb 2 oz) raw chicken bones
2 carrots, roughly chopped
1 onion, roughly chopped
2 celery stalks, roughly chopped
½ leek, white part only, roughly
  chopped
5–6 flat-leaf parsley stems
2–3 thyme sprigs
3 dried bay leaves
10 black peppercorns

CUSTARD

1 teaspoon olive oil
125 ml (4 fl oz/½ cup) full-cream
  (whole) milk
125 ml (4 fl oz/½ cup) thick
  (double/heavy) cream
2 eggs
4 egg yolks
pinch of salt
pinch of freshly grated nutmeg

MEATBALLS

100 g (3½ oz) minced (ground) beef
100 g (3½ oz) minced (ground) pork
½ onion, grated
25 g (1 oz/⅓ cup) fresh
  breadcrumbs

This soup is traditionally served as a starter at German weddings, but it's certainly hearty enough to make a main meal for two.

To make the broth, place all of the ingredients in a large saucepan and cover with 3 litres (101 fl oz/12 cups) cold water. Bring to the boil, then reduce the heat and simmer for 1½ hours, removing any scum that rises to the surface during cooking. Remove from the heat and set aside for 30 minutes to cool slightly. Strain the broth twice through muslin (cheesecloth) and discard the solids. Place in the fridge to cool completely, then remove the fat from the surface and discard.

To make the custard, preheat the oven to 150°C (300°F). Grease a 21 cm x 11 cm (8¼ in x 4¼ in) baking dish or tin with the oil, then line with baking paper. Heat the milk and cream in a small saucepan over medium heat until hot, but not boiling. Remove from the heat and set aside to cool slightly. In a bowl, whisk together the eggs, egg yolks, salt and nutmeg until well combined. Slowly whisk the milk mixture into the beaten egg, then pour into the baking dish – it should come 2 cm (¾ in) up the sides of the dish. Place the dish inside a larger baking tin, then pour in enough boiling water to come halfway up the sides. Bake in the oven for 25–30 minutes, until the custard is set. Set aside to cool, then gently turn out onto a plate. Cut the custard into 12 equal-sized pieces – diamonds are the traditional shape.

To make the meatballs, combine the minced meats, onion and breadcrumbs in a bowl. Season well with salt and freshly ground black pepper then, using your hands, knead until well combined. Take 1 tablespoonful of the mixture and roll it into a meatball. Repeat with the remaining mixture until you have approximately 16 meatballs.

To assemble, bring two saucepans of water to the boil. Add the asparagus, peas and carrot to one pan and the pasta to the other pan. Simmer the vegetables for 4–5 minutes until tender, then remove with a slotted spoon. Add the meatballs to the pan, then reduce to a simmer and cook for 5–7 minutes until cooked through. Cook the pasta until al dente, then drain and set aside. Heat the broth in the same saucepan until hot.

Divide the cooked meatballs, egg custard, vegetables and cooked pasta evenly among four shallow soup bowls. Pour over the hot broth, garnish with the parsley and serve.

KARTOFFELSUPPE

POTATO SOUP

serves 4

---

15 g (½ oz) butter
2 tablespoons olive oil
1 leek, white part only, sliced
2 carrots, chopped
1 onion, finely chopped
750 g (1 lb 11 oz) potatoes, chopped
  into 2 cm (¾ in) chunks
1 litre (34 fl oz/4 cups) chicken
  stock
100 g (3½ oz) light rye sourdough
  bread (about 2 thick slices)
4 Frankfurter sausages, sliced
  diagonally
large handful flat-leaf parsley,
  chopped, plus extra to serve
90 g (3 oz/⅓ cup) sour cream,
  plus extra to serve

Potato soup is a staple in German kitchens across the country. If you like, replace the chicken stock for vegetable stock and do away with the sausages to make a vegetarian version.

Heat the butter and half the oil in a large heavy-based saucepan over medium heat. Add the leek, carrot and onion and cook, stirring occasionally, for 10 minutes. Add the potato and cook for a further 5 minutes, stirring often, until the potato just starts to take on some colour. Add the stock – it should just cover the vegetables – adding a little water to top it up, if necessary. Bring to the boil, reduce the heat to a simmer, then cover and cook for 15–20 minutes until the potato is tender.

Meanwhile, heat the remaining oil in a large heavy-based frying pan over medium heat. Tear the bread into rough 1.5 cm (½ in) pieces and add to the pan with the sliced sausage. Cook, stirring occasionally, for about 5 minutes until the bread and sausage pieces are well browned and crisp.

Add the parsley to the soup then remove from the heat. Using a hand-held blender, purée the soup to the texture of your liking. Stir in the sour cream and season with salt and freshly ground black pepper.

Serve the soup in large bowls with an extra dollop of sour cream and topped with the croutons and sausage.

ZWIEBELKUCHEN

ONION TART

serves 6

---

30 g (1 oz) butter
2 tablespoons olive oil
3 onions, thinly sliced
sea salt flakes
180 g (6½ oz/¾ cup) sour cream
80 ml (2½ fl oz/⅓ cup) full-cream
   (whole) milk
4 eggs, beaten
pinch of ground white pepper
pinch of ground nutmeg
pinch of sweet paprika
100 g (3½ oz) smoked cheddar-
   style cheese, grated
green salad leaves, to serve

SHORTCRUST PASTRY

225 g (8 oz/1½ cups) plain
   (all-purpose) flour, plus extra
   for dusting
125 g (4½ oz) cold unsalted butter,
   chopped
1 egg yolk
about 1 tablespoon iced water

Typically, this German onion tart is made with diced bacon – much like the French quiche lorraine – but the addition of smoked cheddar imparts a richness, so its addition is optional.

To make the pastry, place the flour and butter in a food processor and pulse until the mixture resembles breadcrumbs. Add the egg yolk and water and process until the ingredients just come together, adding a little more water, if necessary. Press the dough into a flat disc shape, cover with plastic wrap and refrigerate for 30 minutes.

On a lightly floured work surface, roll out the pastry between two sheets of baking paper to 3–4 mm (¼ in) thick and use it to line a 22 cm (8¾ in) loose-based tart (flan) tin. Trim the pastry, allowing a little extra height up the side of the tin to allow for any shrinkage. Chill the pastry in the tin for 30 minutes.

Preheat the oven to 200°C (400°F).

Heat the butter and oil in a large heavy-based frying pan over medium–low heat. Add the onion and season well with salt. Cook, stirring occasionally, for about 20 minutes until soft and fragrant. Set aside to cool.

Line the chilled pastry with baking paper or foil and fill with baking weights, dried beans or rice. Bake for 15 minutes, then remove the weights and paper and bake for a further 5 minutes or until the pastry base is lightly browned. Set aside to cool slightly.

Whisk the sour cream, milk, egg, spices and a pinch of salt together in a large jug until well combined.

Reduce the oven temperature to 180°C (350°F). Spoon the onion into the prepared tart case, scatter evenly with the cheese and pour the egg mixture over the top. Bake for 25 minutes, or until the filling is lightly browned on top and just set.

Remove from the oven and leave to cool in the tin for at least 20 minutes. Serve warm, or at room temperature with a green salad on the side.

WIENERSCHNITZEL

VIENNA-STYLE CRUMBED VEAL CUTLET

serves 4

---

50 g (1¾ oz/⅓ cup) plain (all-purpose) flour
sea salt flakes
2 eggs
140 g (5 oz) fresh breadcrumbs or panko crumbs
2 tablespoons finely chopped flat-leaf parsley, plus extra to serve
4 veal cutlets (about 80 g/2¾ oz each)
1 onion, halved
30 g (1 oz) unsalted butter
2 tablespoons olive oil
caperberries, to serve
lemon cheeks, to serve

As the name suggests, this dish is a classic Viennese recipe made by crumbing and frying flattened veal pieces. It's a hugely popular dish across Germany, too, and has been for the last few centuries! Although it's not traditional, Japanese-style panko crumbs will give the schnitzels a crunchier, more delicious coating.

Place the flour, a generous pinch of sea salt and freshly ground black pepper in a zip-lock bag. Shake the bag to combine. Whisk the eggs in a shallow bowl and combine the breadcrumbs and parsley in another shallow bowl.

Working with one cutlet at a time, place the veal between two sheets of non-stick baking paper. Use a meat mallet or rolling pin to pound the meat gently until it is about 5 mm (¼ in) thick. Rub both sides with the cut side of the onion, then repeat with the remaining pieces of veal.

Add the veal, one piece at a time, to the zip-lock bag and shake to coat in the flour mixture. Shake off the excess flour, then dip in the egg, allowing any excess liquid to drip off, and finally press into the breadcrumbs. Repeat this process with the remaining veal, then cover and refrigerate for 30 minutes.

Heat the butter and oil in a large, heavy-based frying pan until bubbling. Cook the schnitzels, in batches if necessary, for 1–2 minutes on each side or until golden and just cooked through.

Serve the schnitzels with caperberries, lemon cheeks for squeezing over and a scattering of extra parsley. The schnitzels are also fantastic served with Krautsalat (page 52), Kartoffelsalat (page 55) or fries.

SAUERBRATEN

SOUR BEEF ROAST

serves 6

1.2 kg (2 lb 10 oz) beef bolar blade
60 ml (2 fl oz/¼ cup) olive oil
1 medium onion, chopped
2 carrots, chopped
3 celery stalks, chopped
3 tablespoons plain (all-purpose)
    flour
small handful flat-leaf parsley,
    chopped, for garnish
Kartoffelknödel (page 67), to serve

BRINE

250 ml (8½ fl oz/1 cup) apple cider
    vinegar
1 onion, roughly chopped
2 fresh bay leaves
5 juniper berries
2 teaspoons sea salt flakes
½ teaspoon black peppercorns
5 cloves

Sauerbraten is a German pot roast, typically made with beef, but can also be made using lamb or pork. Note that you need to start this recipe three days in advance, but your reward will be the most tender, juicy and moreish roast you'll ever eat.

To make the brine, place all of the ingredients along with 500 ml (17 fl oz/ 2 cups) water in a medium-sized saucepan over high heat. Bring to the boil, then remove from the heat and set aside to cool. Place the beef in a large bowl and pour over the brine. Cover and refrigerate for 3 days, turning the beef twice daily.

Preheat the oven to 180°C (350°F).

Remove the beef from the brine and pat dry. Strain the brine and reserve the liquid. Heat half the oil in a flameproof heavy-based Dutch oven or casserole dish over medium–high heat. Add the beef and cook for 15–20 minutes, turning until seared all over. Transfer to a plate and set aside.

Add the onion, carrot and celery to the Dutch oven and cook for 5 minutes, stirring occasionally. Return the beef to the pan along with the reserved liquid. Cover, and cook for 2–2½ hours, until the beef is very tender. Transfer the beef to a cutting board to rest.

Heat the remaining oil in a small saucepan over medium heat. Add the flour and cook, stirring continuously, until the flour turns brown and gives off a nutty fragrance. Watch the flour closely as it can burn quickly once it starts to change colour. Pour a ladleful of hot stock from the Dutch oven into the roux, stirring until smooth. Add a second ladleful of stock and stir. Pour the thickened sauce into the Dutch oven and stir to combine with the remaining stock and vegetables.

Slice the beef and return to the pan to coat in the hot sauce. Scatter over the parsley and serve with Kartoffelknödel (page 67).

FRIKADELLEN

MEATBALLS

serves 4

---

300 g (10½ oz) minced (ground)
  beef
300 g (10½ oz) minced (ground)
  pork
1 onion, grated
1 egg, beaten
40 g (1½ oz/½ cup) fresh
  breadcrumbs
3 tablespoons chopped dill pickles
2 teaspoons chopped marjoram
1 teaspoon German mustard
1 tablespoon olive oil

CREAMY HORSERADISH SAUCE

2 tablespoons finely grated fresh
  horseradish or 2–3 tablespoons
  jarred horseradish
125 g (4½ oz/½ cup) sour cream
2 tablespoons egg mayonnaise
2 teaspoons sweet German mustard
1 spring onion (scallion), finely
  chopped

**Every country has its own version of meatballs – often a modest
dish created at home and designed for comfort eating. The German
interpretation is no exception. This recipe uses dill pickles and mustard
in the beef and pork balls and serves them with a sharp and creamy
horseradish sauce.**

Combine the minces, onion, egg, breadcrumbs, pickle, marjoram and
mustard in a bowl. Season lightly with salt and freshly ground black pepper.
Mix with damp hands and form into 8 patties. Transfer to a plate, cover and
chill for 30 minutes.

Meanwhile, to make the horseradish sauce, combine all of the ingredients in
a medium-sized bowl. Mix well, taste and season with salt and freshly ground
black pepper, if necessary. Cover and set aside in the fridge until required.

Heat the oil in a large heavy-based frying pan over medium–high heat.
Add the burgers, flatten slightly with the back of a spatula and cook for
8–10 minutes, until well crusted and browned on both sides.

Transfer to serving plates and serve with the horseradish sauce.

JÄGERSCHNITZEL

HUNTER'S CUTLET

serves 4

90 g (3 oz) plain (all-purpose) flour
1 teaspoon salt
1 teaspoon freshly ground black
   pepper
1 teaspoon garlic powder
3 eggs
240 g (8½ oz/3 cups) finely milled
   fresh breadcrumbs
2 tablespoons flat-leaf parsley,
   chopped, for garnish
4 pork cutlets (about 100 g/
   3½ oz each)
60 ml (2 fl oz/¼ cup) vegetable oil

MUSHROOM SAUCE

20 g (¾ oz) butter
1 teaspoon olive oil
200 g (7 oz) bacon slices, sliced
   into batons
½ small onion, finely chopped
1 garlic clove, crushed
200 g (7 oz) button mushrooms,
   sliced
2 tablespoons plain (all-purpose)
   flour
125 ml (4 fl oz/½ cup) red wine
375 ml (12½ fl oz/1½ cups)
   beef stock
125 ml (4 fl oz/½ cup) thick
   (double/heavy) cream

Jägerschnitzel can be found in many delicious variations across Germany. The dish typically uses pork (as with this recipe), but can also be made with veal, turkey or chicken. Some versions skip the breaded coating altogether, while others coat the meat in mustard. The one essential part to Jägerschnitzel, however, is the creamy mushroom sauce you serve it with.

Place the flour, salt, pepper and garlic powder in a zip-lock bag. Shake the bag to combine. Whisk the eggs in a shallow bowl and combine the breadcrumbs and parsley in another shallow bowl.

Working with one cutlet at a time, place the pork between two sheets of non-stick baking paper. Use a meat mallet or rolling pin to pound the meat gently until it is about 1 cm (½ in) thick.

Add the pork, one cutlet at a time, to the zip-lock bag and shake to coat in the flour mixture. Shake off the excess flour, then dip in the egg, allowing any excess liquid to drip off, and finally press into the breadcrumb mixture. Repeat this process with the remaining pork cutlets, then cover and refrigerate for 30 minutes.

To make the sauce, heat the butter and olive oil in a frying pan over high heat and add the bacon. Cook until crisp, then remove with a slotted spoon and set aside to drain on paper towel. Remove all but 1 tablespoon of fat from the pan, then reduce the heat to medium and add the onion, garlic and mushrooms. Fry for 3–4 minutes, stirring occasionally, until softened. Return half of the bacon to the pan and add the flour. Cook for 1–2 minutes, then add the red wine. Cook for 2–3 minutes, until the wine has reduced by one-third, then add the stock. Continue to reduce the sauce for a further 5–7 minutes, until again reduced by one-third. Finally, add the cream and cook for 5 minutes, or until the sauce has thickened.

Heat the vegetable oil in a frying pan over medium heat and add 2 cutlets. Cook for 4–5 minutes on each side, then remove from the pan and drain on paper towel. Repeat with the remaining cutlets.

Serve each cutlet with a large spoonful of sauce poured over the top. Garnish with the remaining bacon and a scattering of parsley.

GÄNSEBRATEN

ROAST GOOSE

serves 6

4 kg (8 lb 13 oz) fresh goose,
  with giblets (you only want
  the liver)
sea salt flakes
freshly ground white pepper
2 onions, peeled and quartered
6 green apples
250 ml (8½ fl oz/1 cup) chicken
  stock
2 tablespoons redcurrant jelly
1 tablespoon red wine vinegar
Kartoffelknodel (page 67) and
  Rotkohl (page 64), to serve

STUFFING

2 tablespoons olive oil
1 onion, finely chopped
110 g (4 oz/2 cups) fresh sourdough
  breadcrumbs
60 g (2 oz/½ cup) redcurrants,
  stalks removed
handful flat-leaf parsley, finely
  chopped
1 teaspoon lemon zest
5 juniper berries, lightly cracked

Roast goose is traditionally served for Christmas lunch alongside cooked red cabbage and potato dumplings. It makes a delicious alternative to roast turkey, as it has a much richer flavour and can be simpler to cook. For the tastiest result, choose a fresh, free-range goose that is plump, with umblemished, pale skin and a good layer of fat.

Preheat the oven to 180°C (350°F).

To prepare the goose, first remove the giblets (which may be in a bag in the cavity), and then wash the goose in cold water, inside and out. Pat dry thoroughly. Trim the excess skin from the neck, and remove the wingtips with kitchen scissors. Remove the fat from inside the cavity, then rub the goose inside and out with sea salt flakes and freshly ground white pepper.

To prepare the stuffing, heat the oil in a small frying pan over medium heat and add the onion. Cook, stirring frequently, for 5 minutes or until softened. Transfer the onion to a mixing bowl.

Half-fill a small saucepan with water and bring to a simmer over low heat. Add the goose liver and blanch for 1 minute, then transfer to a chopping board. When cool enough to handle, chop the liver finely and add to the onion, along with the breadcrumbs, redcurrants, parsley, lemon zest and juniper berries. Season with salt and pepper and mix to combine. Fill the goose cavity loosely with the stuffing, then pull the skin over to enclose and secure with toothpicks.

To help release excess fat during cooking, use a fine skewer to pierce the skin, but not the meat of the goose, particularly around the legs and thighs.

Place a wire rack in a roasting tin and add 500 ml (17 fl oz/2 cups) boiling water. Place the goose, breast side up, on the rack and transfer to the oven. Cook for 30 minutes, then remove from the oven and turn the goose onto one side. Baste with the pan juices, then cook for a further 30 minutes.

Place the quartered onion and the apples in the roasting tin and baste with the pan juices. Turn the goose on to its other side and baste again. Excess fat from the pan can be easily removed with a turkey baster. Return to the oven for 30 minutes.

Turn the goose breast side up again and baste. Turn the onion and apples, and cook for a further 45 minutes, or until the juice runs clear when the thickest part of the thigh is pierced with a skewer. Remove from the oven, cover the goose loosely with foil and allow to rest for 30 minutes.

Transfer the goose, apple and onion to a large serving platter. Remove the excess fat from the roasting tin and place on the stovetop over medium heat. Deglaze the pan with the chicken stock, then add the redcurrant jelly and vinegar. Simmer to reduce, then strain and transfer to a serving jug.

Serve the goose with Kartoffelknödel (page 67) and Rotkohl (page 64).

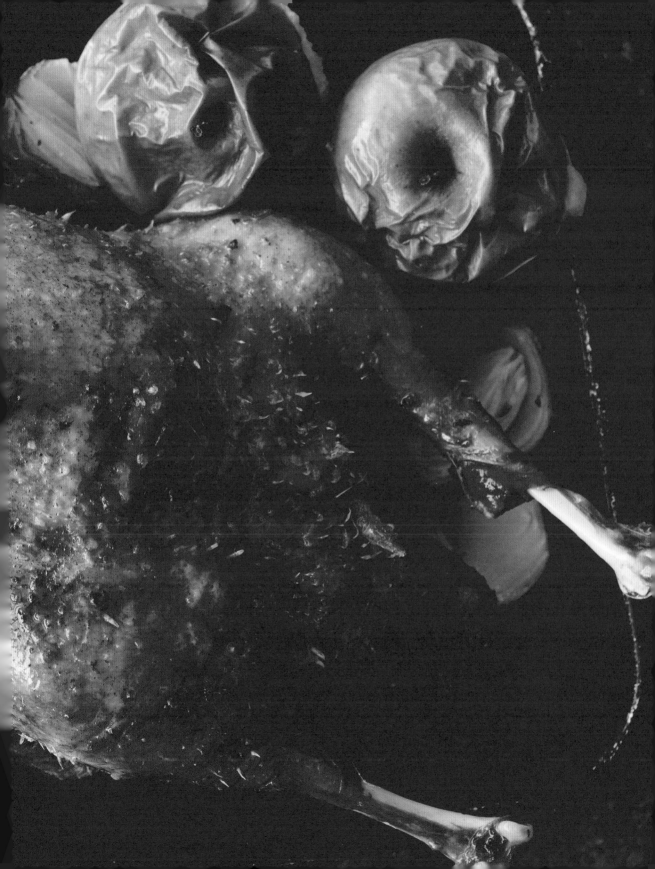

KÖNIGSBERGER KLOPSE

MEATBALLS WITH A CREAMY CAPER SAUCE

serves 4

1 litre (34 fl oz/4 cups) beef stock
1 carrot, chopped
1 small onion, quartered
1 fresh bay leaf
boiled potatoes, to serve
pickled beetroot (beets), to serve

MEATBALLS

20 g (¾ oz) butter
1 small onion, finely chopped
80 g (2¾ oz) (about 2 slices)
   stale bread
250 g (9 oz) minced (ground) veal
250 g (9 oz) minced (ground) pork
zest of ½ lemon
3 anchovy fillets, mashed
1 egg

CREAMY CAPER SAUCE

40 g (1½ oz) butter
2 tablespoons plain (all-purpose)
   flour
juice of ½ lemon
1 tablespoon dry white wine
60 g (2 oz) baby capers, drained
¼ teaspoon sugar
90 g (3 oz/⅓ cup) sour cream
1 egg yolk

Reputed to have originated some 200 years ago, this recipe for meatballs in a creamy sour cream and caper sauce shows no sign of losing its appeal across Germany. And rightfully so. Serve it the German way with boiled potatoes and pickled beetroot, to help to cut through the richness of the sauce.

To prepare the meatballs, melt the butter in a small saucepan over low heat. Add the onion and cook for 4–5 minutes or until soft and translucent. Remove from the heat and set aside to cool.

Meanwhile, briefly soak the bread in a small bowl of water, then remove and squeeze out any excess water.

Add the onion and bread to a mixing bowl along with the minced veal and pork, lemon zest, mashed anchovies, egg and a good grinding of black pepper. Mix together by hand until thoroughly combined. Using wet hands, roll tablespoons of the mixture into balls – you should have 25–30 in total.

Heat the beef stock in a large saucepan over medium heat and add the carrot, onion and bay leaf. When the liquid starts to simmer, gently add the meatballs. Cover and simmer for 10–12 minutes. Remove from the heat and allow to stand, covered, for 5 minutes.

Using a slotted spoon, remove the meatballs, transfer to a plate and cover to keep warm. Strain and reserve the liquid.

To make the creamy caper sauce, melt the butter in a saucepan over low heat and stir in the flour. Continue to stir for 1–2 minutes, then add 375 ml (12½ fl oz/1½ cups) of the reserved cooking liquid, 125 ml (4 fl oz/½ cup) at a time, stirring rapidly until smooth after each addition. Stir in the lemon juice, wine, capers and sugar, and heat the sauce until simmering.

Use a fork to beat the sour cream and egg yolk together in a small bowl. Remove the pan from the heat and stir the cream and egg mixture into the sauce. Add the meatballs to the sauce and stir gently to coat.

Serve immediately with hot boiled potatoes and pickled beetroot.

HOLSTEINER HÜHNERSCHNITZEL

HOLSTEIN-STYLE CRUMBED CHICKEN CUTLET

serves 4

---

2 x 250 g (9 oz) skinless chicken breast fillets
50 g (1¾ oz/⅓ cup) plain (all-purpose) flour
sea salt flakes
6 eggs
140 g (5 oz/1¾ cups) fresh breadcrumbs
35 g (1¼ oz/⅓ cup) grated parmesan
60 ml (2 fl oz/¼ cup) olive oil
100 g (3½ oz) unsalted butter
8 anchovy fillets, drained
1 tablespoon finely chopped flat-leaf parsley
1 tablespoon chopped capers
juice of 1 lemon

This classic schnitzel recipe has its origins in nineteenth century Berlin, when the restaurant Borchardt created the dish to curry favour with the influential civil servant Friedrich von Holstein. The dish remains on the restaurant's menu today.

Cut each chicken breast fillet in half horizontally. You should end up with 4 pieces of chicken roughly the same size. Place the chicken between two sheets of non-stick baking paper. Use a meat mallet to gently pound the fillets to about 1 cm (½ in) thick.

Place the flour, a generous pinch of sea salt and freshly ground black pepper in a zip-lock bag. Shake well to combine. Whisk 2 of the eggs in a shallow bowl and combine the breadcrumbs and parmesan in another shallow bowl.

Add the chicken, two pieces at a time, to the zip-lock bag and shake to coat in the flour mixture. Shake off the excess flour. Dip the chicken in the egg, allowing any excess liquid to drip off, then finally press into the breadcrumb mixture. Cover, and refrigerate for 30 minutes.

Heat 2 tablespoons of the oil and 40 g (1½ oz) of the butter in a heavy-based frying pan. Cook the schnitzels, in batches if necessary, until golden and cooked through, adding a little more oil to the pan if required. Transfer the schnitzels to a plate, cover and keep warm. Wipe the pan clean.

Return the pan to the heat and add the remaining oil. Crack the remaining eggs in the pan and fry until cooked to your liking. Place an egg on each schnitzel and lay 2 anchovies in a criss-cross pattern over each egg.

Return the pan to the heat and add the remaining butter. Cook, swirling, for about 30 seconds until brown and nutty. Stir in the parsley, capers and lemon juice, then pour over the schnitzels and eggs.

Serve the schnitzels with Weisskrautsalat (page 52), Kartoffelsalat (page 55) or Spätzle (page 56).

PILZSTRUDEL MIT ZIEGENKÄSE

MUSHROOM STRUDEL WITH GOAT'S CHEESE

serves 6 as an entrée or 4 as a main meal

---

60 g (2 oz) butter
1 garlic clove, crushed
500 g (1 lb 2 oz) Swiss brown
  mushrooms, roughly chopped
1 teaspoon chopped thyme leaves
1 tablespoon chopped flat-leaf
  parsley
2 teaspoons plain (all-purpose)
  flour
sea salt flakes
100 g (3½ oz) goat's cheese,
  crumbled
6 sheets filo pastry
green salad leaves, to serve

This recipe combines the classic flavours of mushroom and goat's cheese with thyme and parsley. It's a simple dish to make – just ensure that the mixture held in the pastry isn't too wet; otherwise it could seep out.

Preheat the oven to 180°C (350°F).

Melt 20 g (¾ oz) of the butter in a frying pan over medium heat. Add the garlic, mushrooms and thyme and cook, stirring frequently, for 5 minutes or until the mushrooms are soft and there is still a little moisture in the base of the pan. Add the parsley and flour, and season with sea salt flakes and freshly ground black pepper. Stir well to combine and cook for a further 1–2 minutes to cook out the flour taste. Remove from the heat and set aside to cool. Gently stir through the goat's cheese.

Melt the remaining butter in a small saucepan. On a clean work surface, lay out 1 filo sheet and brush with melted butter. Top with the remaining sheets, buttering between each layer.

Place the mushroom filling along the long base of the filo sheets, allowing a little room at each end to fold the pastry over to enclose.

Roll the mixture in the filo, and tuck the ends under at the sides. Brush with melted butter, then make deep parallel diagonal cuts in the top. Transfer to a baking tray.

Bake for 20–25 minutes, until golden brown. Slice and serve warm with a green salad.

EISBEIN MIT SAUERKRAUT

ROAST PORK KNUCKLE WITH FERMENTED CABBAGE

serves 4

4 pork knuckles
3 onions, roughly chopped
3 carrots, roughly chopped
2 celery stalks, roughly chopped
4 dried bay leaves
20 black peppercorns
6 juniper berries
20 g (¾ oz) salt, plus extra
   for rubbing
200 g (7 oz) Sauerkraut (page 63)
mashed potato, to serve

BRINE

salt
5–6 juniper berries (optional)

ONION AND ROSEMARY GRAVY

20 g (¾ oz) butter
1 tablespoon olive oil
1 onion, thinly sliced
½ teaspoon chopped rosemary
2 tablespoons plain (all-purpose)
   flour
500 ml (17 fl oz/2 cups) chicken
   stock

Pork knuckle may not be a common cut you'll find at your butcher – so you'll have to seek it out – but it is well-loved in Germany. The secret to getting a succulent, flavoursome end result is the two-day brining process before you start cooking – it's definitely worth the effort.

Place the knuckles in a large container that will fit in your fridge, ensuring that they can be completely submerged.

To make the brine, measuring as you go, add enough cold water to completely submerge the knuckles. Based on how much water you've used, calculate how much salt you need – every 1 litre (34 fl oz/4 cups) of water requires 155 g (5½ oz/½ cup) of salt. Transfer 600 ml (21½ fl oz) of the water to a saucepan, then add the salt quantity that matches the entire amount of water and the juniper berries, if using. Bring to the boil, stirring to ensure that the salt dissolves, then transfer to the fridge to cool completely. Pour back into the container with the knuckles, then cover and leave for 2 days, checking to ensure that the knuckles stay submerged.

Using a pair of kitchen scissors, prepare the pork knuckles by making 1 cm (½ in) long cuts into the pork skin around the base of the knuckle, about 2 cm (¾ in) apart.

If you don't have a saucepan large enough to fit the pork knuckles together, divide 2 of the onions and carrots, 1 celery stalk, 2 bay leaves, the peppercorns, juniper berries and table salt between two smaller pans. Place the knuckles in the saucepans and cover with cold water. Bring to the boil, then reduce to a simmer and cook for 1–1½ hours. After 1 hour of cooking, test the knuckles by pushing a meat knife into the pork – if the meat slides off the knife easily, they are done. If there is still a little resistance, continue cooking for up to a further 30 minutes.

Remove the knuckles from the pans and set aside to cool slightly. Pat dry with paper towel. Strain the cooking liquid, reserving half of the total liquid.

continued over the page

Preheat the oven to 180°C (350°F).

Use a sharp knife to score the skin around the knuckles. Rub up to 1½ teaspoons salt into the skin of each knuckle.

Place the remaining onion, carrot and bay leaves in a roasting tin and add 500 ml (17 fl oz/2 cups) of the reserved cooking liquid. Place the knuckles on a wire rack over the roasting tin, and carefully transfer to the oven. Cook for 1 hour, basting with the reserved liquid. After 1 hour, use a meat thermometer to check that the internal temperature is above 70°C (160°F). If it isn't, continue to roast, checking every 15 minutes. Once it has reached 70°C (160°F), carefully remove the liquid from the base of the tin and discard. Return the knuckles to the oven and increase the temperature to 230°C (450°F). Roast for a further 30 minutes until the skin has turned into crisp crackling.

Remove from the oven and cover with foil while you make the gravy.

Heat the butter and oil in a frying pan over medium–high heat. Add the onion and cook for 5–7 minutes, stirring occasionally, until golden brown. Add the rosemary and flour, and cook for 1–2 minutes. Add the stock and stir well. Cook for 3–4 minutes, stirring, until the gravy has thickened, then season well with salt and freshly ground black pepper.

Serve the pork knuckles with mashed potato and sauerkraut with the onion and rosemary gravy poured over the top.

ROULADEN

ROLLED AND STUFFED BEEF

serves 4

---

4 x 150 g (5½ oz) pieces beef
  topside
sea salt flakes
ground white pepper
1 medium onion, thinly sliced
150 g (5½ oz) streaky bacon, sliced
  into thin strips
1 medium carrot, sliced into thin
  strips
2 tablespoons olive oil
125 ml (4 fl oz/½ cup) red wine
250 ml (8½ fl oz/1 cup) tomato
  passata (puréed tomatoes)
½ teaspoon mild mustard
2 tablespoons plain (all-purpose)
  flour
mashed potato, to serve
Rotkohl (page 64), to serve

This rich and comforting beef dish can also be served with Spätzle (page 56) instead of mashed potato, as they both help to soak up the rich gravy. To add a little more tang to the dish, chop up a few dill pickles and add them to the onion, bacon and carrot filling.

Working with one piece of beef at a time, place the meat between two pieces of plastic wrap and pound using a meat mallet or rolling pin until it is approximately 3–4 mm (¼ in) thick. Take care to avoid making holes in the beef. Cut each schnitzel in half, widthways.

To make the rouladen, lay the flattened beef pieces on a clean work surface and season each lightly with sea salt flakes and white pepper. Cover the lower two-thirds of each piece with a layer of onion, bacon and carrot, then roll up tightly and secure with skewers.

Heat the oil in a large heavy-based frying pan over medium–high heat. Cook the rouladen, in batches if necessary, for 10–12 minutes, turning frequently, until brown all over. Transfer to a large heavy-based saucepan with a lid.

Deglaze the frying pan with the wine and 500 ml (17 fl oz/2 cups) water, scraping the base over low heat to loosen all the browned meat and juices. Pour over the rouladen in the saucepan. Add the tomato passata and mustard. Cover and cook over low heat for 1½–2 hours, until the beef is very tender, adding additional water as required.

Whisk the flour with 80 ml (2¾ fl oz/⅓ cup) water. Remove the rouladen from the sauce and stir in the flour mixture. Simmer, stirring for a few minutes, until the sauce has thickened. Adjust the seasoning, to taste, and return the rouladen to the sauce and heat through.

Serve the rouladen with mashed potato and Rotkohl (page 64).

CHAPTER FOUR

DESSERTS

APFELKUCHEN

APPLE CAKE

serves 8

---

125 g (4½ oz) unsalted butter,
  softened, plus extra for greasing
115 g (4 oz/½ cup) caster
  (superfine) sugar
1 teaspoon vanilla extract
150 g (5½ oz/1 cup) plain
  (all-purpose) flour
1½ teaspoons baking powder
pinch of salt
1 egg, beaten

APPLE TOPPING

2 apples, peeled, cored and sliced
  into thin wedges
1 teaspoon ground cinnamon
½ teaspoon mixed (pumpkin pie)
  spice
finely grated zest of ½ lemon
juice of 1 lemon
2 tablespoons demerara sugar

As you would expect for a country with a diverse landscape and long culinary history, there are dozens of variations of the humble German apple cake. Some versions include yeast, which causes the cake to rise, while others spike the batter with rum. This recipe uses a simple cake batter and tops it with the classic flavours of apple, cinnamon and sugar.

Preheat the oven to 180°C (350°F). Line the base of a 20 cm (8 in) springform cake tin with baking paper and grease the side of the tin with butter.

To make the topping, combine the apple, spices, lemon zest and juice and half of the sugar in a mixing bowl. Set aside.

Cream the butter, sugar and vanilla in the bowl of an electric mixer until light and pale. Sift the flour, baking powder and salt into the bowl, add the egg and beat until just combined. Spread evenly into the prepared tin.

Arrange the apple decoratively, in two concentric circles, on top of the cake mixture. Drizzle over any remaining juice from the bowl and sprinkle with the remaining sugar.

Bake for 40–45 minutes, until the top is lightly browned and a skewer inserted into the centre of the cake comes out clean. Cool in the tin for 15 minutes before turning out onto a wire rack.

Serve the cake warm or cold. It is best eaten on the day it is made.

APFEL-RHABARBER STRUDEL

APPLE AND RHUBARB STRUDEL

serves 10

---

125 g (4½ oz) butter
16 sheets filo pastry
icing (confectioners') sugar,
  to serve
whipped cream, to serve

FILLING

3 apples, peeled, cored
  and finely chopped
1 tablespoon lemon juice
4 rhubarb stalks, thinly sliced
110 g (4 oz/½ cup) sugar
40 g (1½ oz/½ cup) fresh
  breadcrumbs
½ teaspoon ground cinnamon

We can thank the German language for the word 'strudel', which describes a layered pastry encasing a (usually, but not always) sweet filling. Apfelstrudel (apple strudel) is the most common version you'll find. This version is a variation on the classic, combining the flavours of apple and rhubarb to create a deeply satisfying dessert. Don't forget to serve it with mounds of whipped cream.

To prepare the filling, combine the apple and lemon juice in a bowl. Add the rhubarb, sugar, breadcrumbs and cinnamon and mix well.

Preheat the oven to 180°C (350°F). Line a large baking tray with baking paper.

Melt the butter in a small saucepan.

Lay 2 sheets of filo pastry side by side on a clean work surface. Brush with a little melted butter then place another 2 sheets on top. Repeat this process until all the pastry has been used. Divide the filling between the pastry squares, leaving a 10 cm (4 in) border at the base and sides. One by one, gently roll the strudels, stopping halfway to fold in the edges, and then roll to the end.

Transfer the strudels to the baking tray. Brush with melted butter and bake for 1 hour or until golden brown.

Remove from the oven and rest for 10 minutes. Dust with icing sugar, then slice and serve warm with whipped cream.

The strudels are best eaten on the day they are made, but they can be reheated in a hot oven for about 10 minutes until crisp the following day.

SCHWARZWÄLDER KIRSCHTORTE

BLACK FOREST CAKE

serves 12–14

---

900 ml (30½ fl oz) thickened cream
1½ sheets gold-strength gelatine,
   soaked in cold water for
   15 minutes
30 g (1 oz/¼ cup) icing
   (confectioners') sugar
1 teaspoon vanilla extract
1 tablespoon Kirsch
fresh cherries, for garnish
60 g (2 oz/½ cup) dark chocolate
   curls or shavings, for garnish

PASTRY BASE

150 g (5½ oz/1 cup) plain
   (all-purpose) flour
1½ tablespoons Dutch processed
   cocoa powder
1 teaspoon baking powder
55 g (2 oz/¼ cup) caster
   (superfine) sugar
1 teaspoon vanilla extract
90 g (3 oz) unsalted butter,
   softened, plus extra for greasing

Could there be a more iconic German dessert than Black Forest cake? Chocolate sponge, cherries, thick cream and dark chocolate shavings – what's not to love? The Black Forest, in Germany's Southwest, is rightly famous for its Morello cherries and Kirsch (a double-distilled cherry liquor). For the best-tasting cake, search out a good-quality Kirsch and avoid any synthetic versions.

Preheat the oven to 180°C (350°F). Line the base of a 25 cm (10 in) springform cake tin.

To make the pastry base, sift the flour, cocoa and baking powder into a mixing bowl. Add the sugar, vanilla and butter and knead by hand for 5 minutes or until a smooth dough forms. Press the dough evenly into the base of the prepared tin (it should be about 6 mm/¼ in thick) and prick several times with a fork. Bake for 15 minutes. Remove the tin from the oven and turn the pastry base out onto a wire rack to cool.

Reduce the oven temperature to 160°C (320°F).

Clean the cake tin and grease the base and side. Line the base with baking paper.

To make the chocolate sponge, place the eggs and sugar in the bowl of an electric mixer and whisk on high speed for 6–7 minutes, until very thick and pale.

Sift the flour, cornflour, cocoa, baking powder and salt twice, and then fold into the egg mixture with a spatula. Work quickly and lightly to retain the air that has been whipped into the eggs. Pour the mixture into the prepared tin and bake for 30 minutes, or until a skewer inserted into the centre of the cake comes out clean. Remove the sponge from the oven and set aside on a wire rack to cool. Gently remove the outer ring from the tin, and allow the sponge to cool before peeling off the baking paper and cutting the sponge in half horizontally.

continued over the page

CHOCOLATE SPONGE

5 eggs
115 g (4 oz/½ cup) caster
   (superfine) sugar
110 g (4 oz/¾ cup) plain
   (all-purpose) flour
30 g (1 oz/¼ cup) cornflour
   (cornstarch)
30 g (1 oz/¼ cup) Dutch processed
   cocoa powder
1 teaspoon baking powder
¼ teaspoon salt

CHERRY FILLING

350 g (12½ oz) tinned or jarred
   Morello cherries, drained, juice
   reserved
2 tablespoons Kirsch
250 ml (8½ fl oz/1 cup) cherry juice
   (from the Morello cherry jar)
3 teaspoons arrowroot powder
1 tablespoon sugar

To make the cherry filling, place the cherries and Kirsch in a bowl and stir to combine. In another bowl, combine 60 ml (2 fl oz/¼ cup) of the cherry juice with the arrowroot and stir until smooth. Heat the remaining cherry juice and the sugar in a small saucepan over medium heat until almost simmering. Add the dissolved arrowroot mixture and stir over medium–low heat until it starts to bubble. Allow it to simmer for 1 minute, then stir in the Kirsch-soaked cherries and remove from the heat. Set aside to cool completely.

Place 125 ml (4 fl oz/½ cup) of the cream in a small saucepan over low heat and warm gently. Squeeze the excess water from the gelatine leaves and add them to the cream. Stir until the gelatine has dissolved, then immediately remove from the heat to cool a little. Place the remaining cream, the icing sugar and vanilla in the bowl of an electric mixer and whip until it starts to thicken. Add the cooled gelatine mixture and continue to whip until firm.

To assemble the cake, place the pastry base onto a cake stand. Sprinkle over a little Kirsch, then spread one-quarter of the cream over the base, leaving a 2 cm (¾ in) border around the edge. Spoon the cherry filling onto the cream, reserving the leftover sauce – the filling will move out to the edge due to the weight of the upper layers.

Place the top half of the sponge cake on the cherries, crumb side down. Sprinkle with a few more drops of Kirsch and spread with another one-quarter of the remaining cream. Place the bottom half of the sponge onto the cream, crumb side down. Sprinkle again with a few drops of Kirsch and spread the remaining cream evenly on the top and side of the cake. Garnish with fresh cherries and scatter the chocolate curls or shavings over the top. If you like, drizzle with some of the leftover sauce.

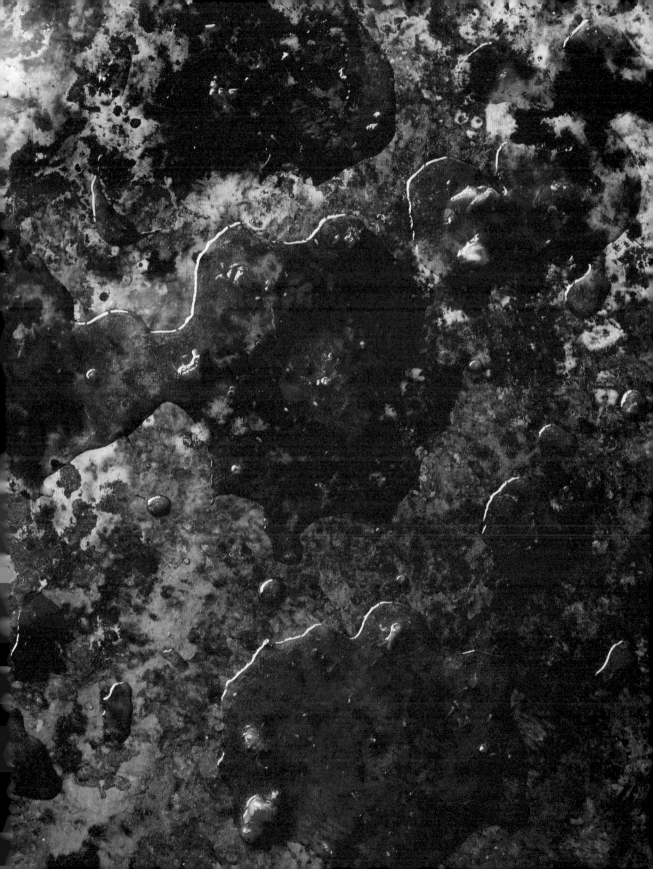

STOLLEN

CHRISTMAS FRUIT CAKE

makes 1 loaf

75 g (2¾ oz) raisins
60 g (2 oz/⅓ cup) mixed peel
60 ml (2 fl oz/¼ cup) bourbon or
   dark rum
1½ teaspoons instant dried yeast
3 tablespoons caster
   (superfine) sugar
80 ml (2½ fl oz/⅓ cup) full-cream
   (whole) milk, warmed
250 g (9 oz/1⅔ cups) plain
   (all-purpose) flour, sifted,
   plus extra for dusting
1 teaspoon ground cinnamon
½ teaspoon ground cardamom
½ teaspoon ground ginger
1 egg, lightly beaten
½ teaspoon salt
100 g (3½ oz) unsalted butter,
   softened
60 g (2 oz/½ cup) slivered almonds
zest of ½ orange
zest of ½ lemon
125 g (4½ oz) marzipan
40 g (1½ oz) butter, melted, plus
   extra for greasing
icing (confectioners') sugar, to dust

Stollen is a bread-like fruit cake typically made during the Christmas season. It has its origins in the city of Dresden – where it was first mentioned in an official document in 1474! You can break with tradition, of course, and bake this at any time of year.

Combine the raisins, mixed peel and bourbon or rum in a small saucepan over medium heat. Heat gently, then remove from the heat and set aside to cool.

Combine the yeast, 1 tablespoon of the caster sugar and milk in the large bowl of an electric mixer fitted with a dough hook. Set aside for 10 minutes or until the mixture bubbles.

Add the flour, remaining caster sugar, spices and egg to the yeast mixture. Mix at low speed just until the mixture starts to come together. With the mixer running, add the salt and then slowly add the softened butter, 1 teaspoon at time. If the dough seems a bit sticky, add 1–2 more tablespoons of flour. Continue to mix, increasing the speed slightly, for about 8 minutes until a soft, smooth dough forms. Add the almonds, citrus zest and soaked fruit and mix until combined. (Alternatively, the dough can be kneaded by hand on a lightly floured work surface for about 10 minutes.)

Form the dough into a ball and place in a greased bowl. Cover, and set aside to rest in a warm place for 1½–2 hours, until the dough has nearly doubled in size.

Preheat the oven to 180°C (350°F). Line a baking tray with baking paper.

Turn the dough out onto a lightly floured work surface and gently press out to a 30 cm x 22 cm (12 in x 8¾ in) oval. Roll the marzipan into a slightly flattened log, just shorter than the width of the dough, then place it vertically off-centre on the dough. Fold the shorter side of the dough over the marzipan and press lightly to seal, then fold the other side over the top. Place on the prepared tray, cover with plastic wrap and set aside in a warm place for 30–45 minutes, until slightly risen.

Remove the plastic wrap, then bake the stollen for 25–30 minutes, until golden brown and cooked through. Remove from the oven, brush with the melted butter and dust generously with icing sugar. Cool completely before slicing. Stollen will keep in an airtight container for up to 4 days.

PFEFFERNÜSSE

GINGERBREAD COOKIES

makes about 30

---

335 g (12 oz/2¼ cups) plain
  (all-purpose) flour
30 g (1 oz) almond meal
2 teaspoons ground cinnamon
1 teaspoon ground white pepper
¼ teaspoon ground cardamom
¼ teaspoon ground cloves
¼ teaspoon ground ginger
¼ teaspoon ground nutmeg
½ teaspoon bicarbonate of soda
  (baking soda)
pinch of salt
125 g (4½ oz) unsalted butter
110 g (4 oz/½ cup) brown sugar
60 ml (2 fl oz/¼ cup) blackstrap
  molasses
1 egg, lightly beaten

SPICED GLAZE

250 g (9 oz/2 cups) pure icing
  (confectioners') sugar, sifted
¼ teaspoon ground nutmeg
¼ teaspoon ground cloves

These sweet, spiced morsels are addictive. Like Stollen (page 113), these cookies are a traditional Christmas treat, but can also be enjoyed year-round. By making the cookie dough ahead of time and leaving it for at least two hours (preferably overnight), the spices will deepen the flavour of the end result.

Sift the flour, almond meal, spices, bicarbonate of soda and salt into a mixing bowl.

Combine the butter, sugar and molasses in a medium-sized saucepan over medium heat. Cook, stirring, until the sugar has dissolved. Set aside to cool for about 5 minutes or until just warm. Add to the flour mixture along with the egg and mix to form a dough. Cover and refrigerate for at least 2 hours and up to overnight, to firm up and to allow the flavours to develop.

Preheat the oven to 180°C (350°F) and line two baking trays with baking paper.

Roll heaped tablespoons of the dough into balls and place about 3 cm (1¼ in) apart on the prepared baking trays. Bake for 15–18 minutes until just firm to touch and lightly browned on the bottom. Transfer to wire racks to cool.

To make the spiced glaze, combine the icing sugar, spices and 60 ml (2 fl oz/¼ cup) water in a mixing bowl – it should be quite runny, so add a little more water, if necessary. Dip the tops of the cookies in the glaze and place back on the wire racks, allowing the glaze to drip down the sides. Allow to set for about 2 hours.

The cookies will keep in an airtight container for up to 5 days.

BIENENSTICH

BEE STING CAKE

serves 6

---

375 g (13 oz/2½ cups) plain
  (all-purpose) flour, plus extra
  for dusting
55 g (2 oz/¼ cup) caster
  (superfine) sugar
2 teaspoons instant dried yeast
½ teaspoon salt
200 ml (7 fl oz) full-cream
  (whole) milk, warmed
50 g (1¾ oz) unsalted butter,
  melted and cooled, plus extra
  for greasing

FILLING

3 tablespoons custard powder
55 g (2 oz/¼ cup) caster
  (superfine) sugar
1 teaspoon vanilla bean paste
250 ml (8½ fl oz/1 cup) full-cream
  (whole) milk
125 ml (4 fl oz/½ cup) whipping
  cream

TOPPING

30 g (1 oz) unsalted butter
2 tablespoons caster
  (superfine) sugar
2 tablespoons honey
40 g (1½ oz) flaked almonds

The Bee Sting is a classic German yeast-enriched layered cake. The dense cake isn't overly sweet, but is offset with a filling of rich vanilla custard and a honey and almond topping.

Combine the flour, sugar, yeast and salt in a large bowl. Pour in the milk and butter and mix until combined to form a rough, soft dough. Cover the bowl with plastic wrap and set aside for 10 minutes.

Turn the dough out onto a lightly floured work surface and knead for 2–3 minutes until smooth. Place in a lightly oiled bowl, cover with plastic wrap and set aside in a warm place for 60–70 minutes until risen by about half its original size.

Lightly grease a 22 cm (8¾ in) springform cake tin and line the base with baking paper. Turn the dough out onto a lightly floured work surface, knead once or twice, then gently press the dough into a 15 cm (6 in) circle. Transfer to the prepared tin, cover and leave to rest in a warm place for about 1 hour or until the dough reaches the top of the tin.

Meanwhile, to make the filling, combine the custard powder, sugar, vanilla and enough milk (about 3–4 tablespoons) to make a smooth paste in a small saucepan. Stir in the remaining milk. Cook, stirring, over medium heat until the mixture boils and thickens. Simmer for 1 minute or until very thick. Transfer to a bowl, cover the surface with plastic wrap to stop a skin forming, and refrigerate until cold.

Beat the cream in the bowl of an electric mixer until firm peaks form. In a separate bowl, beat the cold custard (it will be very firm) using the electric mixer until smooth, then fold in the cream. Cover and refrigerate until required.

continued over the page

Preheat the oven to 180°C (350°F).

To make the topping, combine the butter, sugar and honey in a small heavy-based saucepan over medium heat and cook, stirring, until the sugar has dissolved. Boil without stirring for about 1½ minutes, until light caramel in colour. Remove from the heat and set aside.

Bake the risen dough in the tin for 30 minutes. Just before the cake is ready, working quickly, reheat the caramel, whisking, to a pourable consistency and stir in the almonds. Spread the cake with the topping, then bake for a further 5 minutes, or until the topping is golden and a skewer inserted into the centre of the cake comes out clean. Remove the cake from the tin and cool on a wire rack.

Slice the cooled cake in half horizontally with a large serrated knife, then spread the base with the prepared filling and top with the remaining cake. It is best eaten as soon as it's ready, although it will store in the fridge for 2–3 hours. It's best to cut the cake with a serrated knife and use a sawing motion, to stop the filling going everywhere!

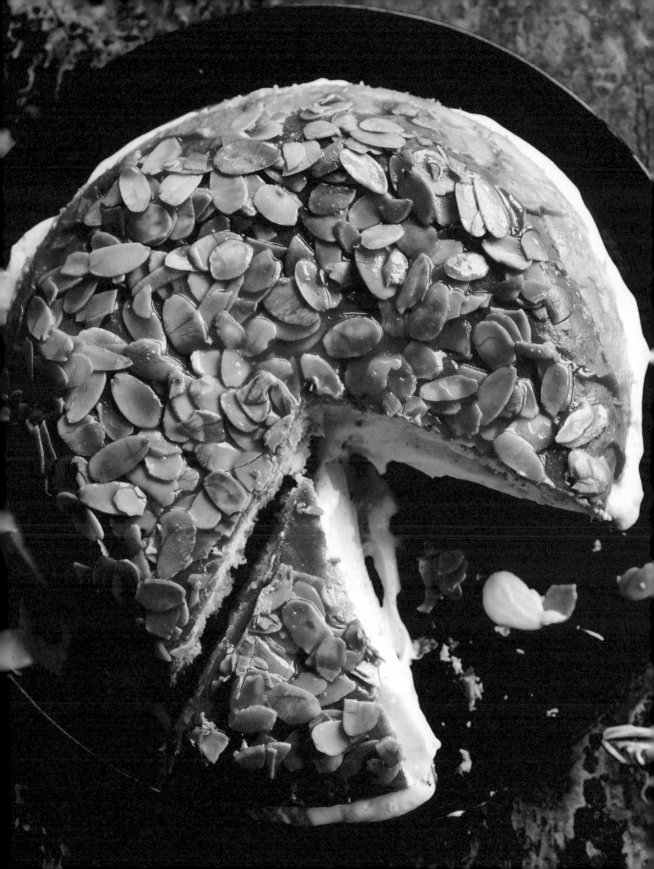

ROTE GRÜTZE

RED FRUIT PUDDING

serves 6

---

500 g (1 lb 2 oz) ripe mixed
   berries, such as raspberries,
   strawberries, red or blackcurrants,
   boysenberries, pitted cherries
   or blueberries (if fresh berries
   are unavailable, use mixed
   frozen berries)
400 ml (13½ fl oz) cherry juice
   (see note)
2 tablespoons lemon juice
2 tablespoons sugar
30 g (1 oz/¼ cup) cornflour
   (cornstarch)

CUSTARD

250 ml (8½ fl oz/1 cup) full-cream
   (whole) milk
1 tablespoon cornflour (cornstarch)
2 strips lemon zest
1 tablespoon sugar

This refreshing, vibrantly red dessert is particularly loved in Northern Germany, where it's often made in summer when red fruits are at their peak. If you like, skip the custard and serve the fruit sauce with ice cream or whipped cream.

Place the fruit, cherry juice, lemon juice and sugar in a medium-sized saucepan over medium heat and bring to the boil. Simmer for 2–3 minutes. Mix the cornflour with 100 ml (3½ fl oz) water and add to the fruit. Cook for a further 2 minutes, stirring constantly, until the mixture resembles a thick sauce. Set aside to cool.

To make the custard, mix 50 ml (1¾ fl oz) of the milk with the cornflour in a small bowl. Heat the remaining milk in a small saucepan with the lemon zest and sugar until just steaming. Remove from the heat and use a slotted spoon to remove the lemon zest. Add the blended cornflour and return to a low heat. Simmer, stirring constantly, for 3–4 minutes. Remove from the heat to cool slightly, stirring occasionally to prevent a skin from forming.

Rote grütze should be served at room temperature.

Note:

• *Cherry juice is available from health food shops and specialty stores.*

PRINZREGENTENTORTE

PRINCE REGENT TORTE

serves 16

---

250 g (9 oz) unsalted butter, softened
275 g (9½ oz) caster (superfine) sugar
2 teaspoons vanilla extract
200 g (7 oz/1⅓ cups) plain (all-purpose) flour
50 g (1¾ oz/⅓ cup) cornflour (cornstarch)
1 teaspoon baking powder
pinch of salt
4 eggs

CHOCOLATE BUTTER CREAM

500 ml (17 fl oz/2 cups) full-cream (whole) milk
1 teaspoon instant coffee powder
80 g (2¾ oz) dark chocolate, chopped
80 g (2¾ oz/⅓ cup) caster (superfine) sugar
2 eggs
50 g (1¾ oz) cornflour (cornstarch)
3 tablespoons Dutch processed cocoa powder, sifted
250 g (9 oz) unsalted butter, softened

GANACHE

300 g (10½ oz/2 cups) chopped dark chocolate
1 tablespoon vegetable oil

Although this is not the quickest cake to prepare – as you need to bake seven layers of sponge – it is not technically complicated and the result is worth the effort. Named after Prince Regent Luitpold, who ruled Bavaria from 1886–1912, the number of layers in the cake reflects the number of governmental districts in the state.

To make the chocolate butter cream, combine the milk and coffee powder in a medium-sized heavy-based saucepan over medium heat and bring just to the boil. Remove from the heat and whisk in the chopped chocolate until melted.

Using a balloon whisk, beat the sugar and eggs together in a large heatproof bowl until well combined, then whisk in the cornflour and cocoa. Keep whisking and slowly pour the hot chocolate milk into the egg mixture and whisk until combined. Return the mixture to the saucepan and cook over medium–low heat, whisking constantly until the mixture thickens and comes to the boil. Simmer for 2 minutes, stirring constantly.

Strain the mixture into a large heatproof bowl and carefully press a piece of plastic wrap over the surface to stop a skin forming. Set aside to cool to room temperature, whisking occasionally. If you want to cool the cream more quickly, whisk the filling over an ice bath.

Beat the butter in the bowl of an electric mixer until smooth. When both mixtures are about the same temperature, add the chocolate cream a spoonful at a time to the butter, mixing well after each addition.

Meanwhile, preheat the oven to 180°C (350°F). Using a 24 cm (9½ in) springform cake tin as a guide, trace a circle around the outside of the tin on a piece of baking paper. Repeat this process until you have seven sheets of baking paper with seven circles.

Cream the butter, sugar and vanilla in the bowl of an electric mixer until light and pale. Sift the flour, cornflour, baking powder and salt into the bowl, add the eggs and beat until combined.

Working with one, two or three layers at a time (depending on the size of your oven), spread just over 125 ml (4 fl oz/½ cup) cake mixture evenly onto the reverse side of each piece of baking paper to the edge of the circle. (Alternatively, weigh the cake mix and divide the amount by seven.) Ensure you spread the mixture evenly, making sure it is not thinner at the edges, as it will overcook.

Bake each cake layer for 8–9 minutes, until cooked through and very lightly browned. Place on a wire rack to cool, then flip over and carefully peel off the baking paper. Repeat until all the cake layers are cooked. Trim any browned or crunchy edges – the layers should all be the same size.

Place one cake layer on a cake board of the same size and, using an off-set spatula, spread with just over 80 ml (2¾ fl oz/⅓ cup) of the butter cream. Repeat with the remaining layers of cake, carefully stacking them as you go. Finally, using a palette knife, spread the side and top of the cake with the remaining butter cream, ensuring it is very smooth. Refrigerate for at least 2–3 hours or overnight, until firm.

To make the ganache, place the chocolate and oil in a heatproof bowl set over a saucepan of simmering water (the bowl should not touch the water). Stir until the chocolate is two-thirds melted, then remove from the heat and continue to stir until completely melted – the chocolate should be warm but not hot. Place the cake on a wire rack over a plate (to catch the drips of chocolate). Pour the ganache onto the top of the cake and spread evenly all over the top and side. If necessary, use a palette knife or off-set spatula to smooth the chocolate, however the less you touch it the smoother it will be.

Allow to set for 1–2 hours, then carefully transfer to a serving plate. Score out portions before cutting with a hot knife.

The finished cake may be refrigerated; however, the ganache will not appear glossy until it warms slightly.

INDEX

Published in 2016 by Smith Street Books
Melbourne | Australia
smithstreetbooks.com

ISBN: 978-1-925418-41-5

CIP data is available from the National Library of Australia

Publisher: Paul McNally
Senior Editor: Lucy Heaver, Tusk studio
Recipe development: Caroline Griffiths, Sue Herold & Aisling Coughlan
Design concept: Kate Barraclough
Design layout: Heather Menzies, Studio31 Graphics
Photographer: Chris Middleton
Art Director & Stylist: Stephanie Stamatis
Food preparation: Caroline Griffiths & Aisling Coughlan

Printed & bound in China by C&C Offset Printing Co., Ltd.

Book 34
10 9 8 7 6 5 4 3 2